Behavior Modification in Therapeutic Recreation:
An Introductory Learning Manual

John Dattilo, Ph.D.
The Pennsylvania State University

and

William D. Murphy, Re.D.
The University of Nebraska

Cover Design by Sandra Sikorski
Library of Congress Catalogue Card Number: 87-51016
ISBN 0-910251-21-5

PREFACE

John Dattilo and William D. Murphy

This learning manual was developed for the purpose of introducing therapeutic recreation specialists to behavior modification and to assist them in developing and strengthening their skills in the application of behavior modification techniques. In addition, the manual may be of value to other professionals who may also find use for the application of behavior modification techniques in leisure settings. It is hoped that this manual will assist therapeutic recreation specialists and other professionals to increase their effectiveness in delivering leisure services.

This self-study manual assumes the reader has no previous knowledge of behavior modification. The manual includes information on (a) describing, observing, and measuring behaviors, (b) understanding behaviors, (c) applying consequences such as positive and negative reinforcement to accelerate behaviors, (d) applying consequences such as extinction, punishment, response cost and time-out from positive reinforcement to decelerate behaviors, (e), teaching behaviors by developing schedules of reinforcement and applying the instructional procedures of shaping and chaining, and (f) facilitating the generalization of behaviors. Each chapter contains a description of the procedures and associated exercises. A series of questions is provided at the end of each chapter. These questions allow the readers to test their acquisition and retention of the previously covered topics. An answer key has been included at the back of the manual to assist readers in evaluating their answers. Many texts were consulted during the development and preparation of this manual to ensure that the information presented is accurate and based on a sound philosophy. These texts and additional references, which can be used for further learning and clarification, are listed at the end of the manual. It is hoped that this manual provides an introduction to behavior modification and stimulates readers to further expand their knowledge and skills in this area.

ACKNOWLEDGEMENTS

The authors would like to express their appreciation to the students and practitioners who diligently worked through earlier drafts of this manual and provided helpful suggestions for improvement and encouragement to complete the project. In addition, the authors would like to thank Larry Adler, Pat Mirenda, and Carol Peterson for their critical review of the manual.

Contents

CHAPTER ONE

INTRODUCTION TO BEHAVIOR MODIFICATION

An understanding of introductory techniques of BEHAVIOR MODIFICATION can provide therapeutic recreation specialists and other professionals with helpful facilitation procedures in the provision of leisure services. The appropriate application of these procedures may allow the therapeutic recreation specialist to more effectively encourage individuals with limitations to participate in recreation activities. However, the application of behavior modification procedures is not restricted to individuals with disabilities or limitations of various kinds. Behavior modification can be used in any setting or circumstance where human beings interact with each other or their environment. Therefore, these procedures may also allow other professionals to assist all recipients of leisure services in enhancing their ability to experience leisure.

Behavior modification is a systematic, performance-based, evaluative method for changing BEHAVIOR. *Behavior* is defined as any observable and measurable act, response or movement by an individual. A behavior that is the focus of programmed efforts aimed at alteration or modification is referred to as a *target behavior*. Behavior modification involves the application of procedures designed to change behavior in a measurable manner. The development of behavior modification originates from the belief that behaviors are LEARNED, rather than inherent, and can thus be altered or modified by additional learning. Behavior modification seeks to avoid inferences, untested hypotheses, vague reasoning, or undefined impulses as explanations for behavior. Whatever the behavior and whatever its cause, the behavior is present in an environment and is influenced and shaped by that environment. Behavior modification focuses on individuals' behaviors. It is the behavior that is the concern and it is behavior that can be changed.

Behavior modification is not a process concerned with attempts to determine the causes of behavior. Instead, the procedures used in behavior modification focus on OBSERVABLE AND MEASURABLE behaviors, rather than presumably influential internal agents.

This approach does not deny the existence of internal agents, but rather concentrates specifically on the observable behaviors which an individual exhibits. Regardless of what is causing the behavior, it is behavior that can be observed and measured. Internal behavioral agents cannot be seen, nor can they be measured with any certainty or precision. Behavior is the focus of behavior modification personnel because it is behavior that can be changed by environmental manipulation.

Behavior modification is based on the premise that humans are reactors to their ENVIRONMENT. The *environment* contains all the circumstances, objects, people, behaviors, and conditions that an individual encounters. The emphasis in behavior modification is placed on the relationship between changes in the environment and changes in the individual's behavior. Through environmental manipulation, modification of an individual's behaviors can occur.

The procedures of behavior modification are very compatible with the PROGRAMMING approach used by therapeutic recreation specialists and other professionals. Based on the needs of participants, professionals develop GOALS AND OBJECTIVES directed toward enhancing the leisure lifestyles of individual participants. The concentration on the use of measurable behaviors in behavior modification facilitates the identification of participant needs and the subsequent development of explicit objectives. These goals and objectives provide direction in determining the delivery of appropriate leisure programs.

Behavior modification procedures should be considered during the PLANNING phase of developing leisure programs and applied during the actual IMPLEMENTATION of the program. Behavior modification techniques provide a means for professionals to assist participants in achieving program objectives by facilitating the acceleration of behaviors that are appropriate in a specific context, while decreasing behaviors that are inappropriate for that context. Application of the principles of behavior modification can facilitate identification of successful intervention techniques. This identification encourages more frequent and systematic application of effective, precise and clear intervention strategies. As a result, behavior modification techniques can be easily incorporated into the existing repertoire of skills possessed by all professionals dedicated to facilitating the leisure experience and can be applied across a variety of settings.

Behavior modification involves the careful observation and analysis of the behaviors of individuals by examining the relationship among behavioral ANTECEDENTS, the BEHAVIORS themselves, and the CONSEQUENCES of these behaviors occurring in the environment. The emphasis in behavior modification on the identification of observable and measurable target behaviors, as well as on the antecedents and consequences of these behaviors, enhances the ability of professionals to conduct systematic program EVALUATION. Conducting effective program evaluation allows the professional to clearly document program effectiveness. Documentation of program effectiveness increases the ability of professionals to demonstrate the provision of quality services and subsequent enhancement of the leisure lifestyles of the participants.

Try the following exercise.

Directions: Identify whether the following statements are TRUE or FALSE by placing a T or an F in the space immediately to the left of the statement.

_____ 1. The implementation of behavior modification principles should be restricted to clinical settings.

_____ 2. A behavior is defined as any observable and measurable act, response or movement by a person.

_____ 3. Behavior modification originates from the belief that many behaviors occur spontaneously, without prior learning.

_____ 4. Behavior modification focuses on measurable and observable behaviors, rather than internal agents.

_____ 5. Behavior modification is primarily concerned with the relationship of the individual's behaviors and associated feelings.

_____ 6. The environment contains all the circumstances, objects, people, behaviors, and conditions that a person encounters.

_____ 7. The professional develops goals and objectives based on the interests and expertise of the existing personnel.

_____ 8. Behavior modification procedures should be considered during the planning, implementation and evaluation phases of a leisure program.

_____ 9. Behavior modification focuses on the individual's behavior and is not concerned with what occurs before or after the target behavior.

_____ 10. Effective program evaluation increase the ability of professionals to document program effectiveness.

Please turn the page to determine the accuracy of your responses.

3

All the statements associated with odd numbers are FALSE and all the statements corresponding to even numbers are TRUE.

In review, the following are CHARACTERISTICS OF BEHAVIOR MODIFICATION:

1. Evaluates methods for changing BEHAVIORS.
2. Originates from the belief the behaviors are LEARNED.
3. Focuses on OBSERVABLE and MEASURABLE behaviors.
4. Based on premise that humans are reactors to the ENVIRONMENT.
5. Is compatible with recreation PROGRAMMING.
6. Should be considered during program PLANNING and IMPLEMENTATION.
7. Focuses on ANTECEDENTS, BEHAVIORS and CONSEQUENCES.
8. Facilitates EVALUATION of behaviors and programs.

You have now completed the introductory material on behavior modification. On the next page you can evaluate how well you retained the information.

TEST YOUR KNOWLEDGE OF AN INTORODUCTION TO BEHAVIOR MODIFICATION

Directions: Please circle the letter corresponding to the best answer.

1. Behavior may be defined as:
   a. a systematic method for changing the environment.
   b. observable and measurable acts, responses, or movements by an individual.
   c. the emotional response of individuals to unfamiliar environments.
   d. the physical movements or actions of an individual.
   e. the presence of internal impulses that cause an individual to act in an inappropriate manner.

2. Behavior modification is a systematic method for:
   a. altering or changing behavior.
   b. determining the causes of behavior.
   c. determining the presence of internal agents.
   d. estimating the effects of behavior in social environments.
   e. identifying inferences that cause specific kinds of behavior.

3. Behavior modification procedures may be used:
   a. in any setting where humans interact with each other or their environment.
   b. only by certified therapeutic recreation specialists.
   c. only in clinical settings.
   d. only with individuals who have emotional limitations.
   e. only with individuals who have physical disabilities.

4. Behavior modification is based on the premise that:
   a. behaviors are determined by internal agents.
   b. behaviors are inherent, rather than learned.
   c. behaviors are learned, rather than inherent.
   d. internal agents are determined by behaviors.
   e. internal agents are determined by environments.

5. A target behavior is a behavior that is:
   a. a model to be adopted by an individual in a behavior modification program.
   b. aimed at modifying the environment.
   c. exhibited by the individual who is applying behavior modification techniques.
   d. the focus of systematic efforts aimed at altering it.
   e. to remain unchanged by an individual in a behavior modification program.

6. Behavior modification focuses on:
   a. hypotheses to be tested.
   b. individuals with disabilities.
   c. inferences.
   d. intenal agents.
   e. observable and measurable behaviors.

7. A basis for behavior modification is the belief that:
   a. change in internal agents can cause change in the environment.
   b. changes in the environment can effect a change in behavior.
   c. internal agents can be measured with the same precision as external agents.
   d. the cause of a behavior must be identified before the behavior can be modified.
   e. it is easier to identify internal agents than it is external agents.

8. Behavior modification emphasizes the concept that:
   a. behavior cannot be influenced by environmental manipulation.
   b. humans are not influenced by their environments.
   c. humans react only to internal agents.
   d. humans react to their environments.
   e. target behaviors must remain unchanged.

9. Behavior modification is based on:
   a. environmental manipulation.
   b. manipulation of internal agents.
   c. the belief that behavior is an inherent trait.
   d. the belief that clinical settings are the best environments for behavior modification procedures to be applied.
   e. the belief that target behaviors must not be changed.

10. Environmental manipulation can facilitate:
    a. change in an individual's behavior.
    b. the determination of causes of behavior.
    c . the measurement of internal agents.
    d. the reduction of the influence of leisure as a determinant
       of lifestyle.
    e. the reduction of the strength of internal agents.

11. Behavior modification procedures are:
    a. compatible with the concept that behaviors are inherent.
    b. compatible with the programming approach used by therapeutic
       recreation specialists.
    c. incompatible with the programming approach used by
       therapeutic recreation specialists.
    d. most useful when applied in clinical settings.
    e. most useful when focused on internal agents.

12. Behavior modification procedures should first be considered
    during the:
    a. acceleration phase of leisure programs.
    b. delivery phase of leisure programs.
    c. evaluation phase of leisure programs.
    d. implementation phase of leisure programs.
    e. planning phase of leisure programs.

13. Behavior modification procedures should:
    a. decrease the strength of behaviors that are appropriate in
       a specific context.
    b. increase the strength of behaviors that are appropriate in
       a specific context.
    c. increase the strength of behaviors that arc inappropriate
       in a specific context.
    d. increase the strength of internal agents.
    e. neutralize the effects of environmental manipulation.

14. Behavior modification techniques are:
    a. easily incorporated into the repertoire of skills possessed
       by recreational professionals.
    b. too sophisticated to be applied by recreation professionals.
    c. useful only in clinical settings.
    d. useful only in natural environments.
    e. useful only when applied to individuals with disabilities.

15. Behavior modification involves the analysis of behaviors and their:
    a. antecedents and consequences.
    b. effect on the environment.
    c. effect on recreation professionals
    d. expression during leisure.
    e. internal causes.

Now that you have completed the evaluation, please check your answers with the ones in the back of the book. If needed, review the introductory material on behavior modification and try the evaluation again. When you are satisfied with your acquisition of the information and understand your errors, turn the page and begin work on the next chapter.

CHAPTER TWO

DESCRIBING BEHAVIORS

The initial step in changing a behavior requires accurate observation and description of the behavior. An accurate description of behavior is dependent upon the use of terms that specify OBSERVABLE and MEASURABLE actions. Picture in your mind a group of hyperactive children. What were the children doing? Were they running around in circles, bouncing up and down, rocking back and forth, or perhaps talking rapidly and gasping for breath? The term "hyperactive" could be applied to any of these actions. However, it would not clearly describe the precise actions or behaviors in which the children were engaging. In this case, "hyperactive" is a label, an interpretation of a group's behavior. In this text, when asked to discuss a behavior, the reader is discouraged from using labels and encouraged to use terms that describe the observable and measurable behavior that is occurring.

Terms that describe behavior must specify actions that are:

1. OBSERVABLE
2. MEASURABLE

Behaviors that are observable and measurable are called *overt* behaviors. OVERT behaviors can be identified with the five senses and, when described, generally mean the same thing to different people. Covert behaviors are not as readily identifiable as overt behaviors. Terms that are applied to indicate covert behaviors are not as specific and may not mean the same thing to different people. *Covert* terms are most often used to describe the interpretations made by an observer about another individual's behavior or attitude and, therefore, may be subject to many different interpretations.

When describing behaviors, observers are often required to write BEHAVIORALLY SPECIFIC statements. *A behaviorally specific* statement is one that depicts explicit actions (overt behaviors). It does not include what the observer assumes the person being observed thinks or feels. It does not refer to covert behaviors, which are subject to many different interpretations. A behaviorally specific statement deals only with actions that are observable and measurable.

9

The following are guidelines for describing behaviors:

1. Use OVERT terms that describe observable and measurable behaviors.
2. Use BEHAVIORALLY SPECIFIC statements to depict explicit actions.

Listed below is a series of terms. In the space provided to the left of the numbers that precede the terms, place a *C* for those that describe covert behaviors and an *O* for those that describe overt behaviors.

_____ 1. laughs _____

_____ 2. talks _____

_____ 3. lazy _____

_____ 4. runs _____

_____ 5. polite _____

_____ 6. depressed _____

_____ 7. selfish _____

_____ 8. smiles _____

_____ 9. screams _____

_____ 10. industrious _____

_____ 11. cries _____

_____ 12. upset _____

_____ 13. indifferent _____

_____ 14. obstinate _____

_____ 15. angry _____

_____ 16. anxious   _____

_____ 17. sad   _____

_____ 18. kicks   _____

_____ 19. throws   _____

_____ 20. apathetic   _____

If you placed a *C* in front of 3, 5-7, 10, 12-17, and 20 you are on the right track! All of these words are subjective interpretations of behaviors or feelings. These terms do not describe directly observable or measurable behaviors; they are covert terms. Because the remaining words are descriptive of specific, concrete actions, they apply to behaviors that are observable and measurable. They are overt terms and should have an *O* placed in front of them.

Now, in the space provided to the immediate right of the COVERT terms, record OVERT actions which may describe the vague COVERT behaviors. If you have difficulty thinking of observable behaviors, review this section.

Once you have completed the exercise, go to the next page and evaluate your understanding of the material presented on describing behaviors.

TEST YOUR KNOWLEDGE OF *DESCRIBING BEHAVIORS*

Directions: Please circle the letter corresponding to the best answer.

1. For a behavior to be considered overt, it must have which of
   the following characteristics?
   a. approachable, observable
   b. approachable, countable
   c. believable, controllable
   d. believable, measurable
   e. observable, measurable

2. What do covert terms describe?
   a. behavioral antecedents
   b. labels and feelings
   c. overt behaviors
   d. precise actions
   e. target behaviors

3. Which of the following is written in behaviorally specific terms?
   a. Betty is angry at Edith.
   b. Cindy stated "I like you" to William.
   c. Jerry does not like Ross.
   d. Larry enjoys being with Diane.
   e. Monica gets upset when she sees Cathy.

4. A label may be described as:
   a. a precise description of an individual's behavior.
   b. a term that depicts a group of specific actions.
   c. an observer's interpretation of an individual's behavior.
   d. essential for depicting overt behavior.
   e. necessary for conveying accurate meaning.

5. Terms used to indicate covert behaviors:
   a. accurately describe the observed individual's feelings.
   b. exclude subjective interpretation.
   c. depict precise actions.
   d. generally mean the same thing to different people.
   e. may not mean the same thing to different people.

6. What is the term used to describe behaviors that are observable and measurable?
   a. antecedents
   b. consequences
   c. covert
   d. feelings
   e. overt

7. Your assistant has described Diane as being an angry person. Which measurable behaviors might your assistant have observed Diane exhibiting?
   a. anxious, hit others, upset
   b. anxious, irritable, unreasonable
   c. hit others, kicked, spit
   d. hot headed, upset, psychotic
   e. illogical, ridiculous, unsatisfied

8. An observer watching the leisure education session said Tyrone was a nice boy with a good attitude. Which measurable behavior might the observer be describing?
   a. attentive.
   b. delighted
   c. interested
   d. smiling
   e. studious

9. Which of the following is a behaviorally specific statement?
   a. Jason is dumb.
   b. Jerry is acting silly.
   c. John is a show-off.
   d. Judy is smart.
   e. June is walking.

10. Five observers were asked to write a statement describing overt behavior on the part of any participant in the recreation center's exercise program. Which of the following is a behaviorally specific statement?
    a. Amy was depressed today.
    b. Carl is a leader.
    c. Denise is extremely intelligent.
    d. Mary threw a ball through the window.
    e. Ralph got angry while playing basketball.

11. Which of the following is a behaviorally specific statement?
    a. Angie argues most of the time.
    b. Cindy attended the baseball game.
    c. James is very active in sports.
    d. Teresa is an outspoken person.
    e. Thomas enjoys playing tennis.

12. Which statement is written in behaviorally specific terms?
    a. Alex was so upset he ran out of the room.
    b. Amy answered the questions correctly.
    c. Carol slammed the door in anger.
    d. Joseph enjoys reading stories every day.
    e. Leon became depressed over the loss of his kids.

13. Which pair of statements is written in behaviorally specific terms?
    a. Ivan is in a world of his own on Saturdays.
       Nathan cried three times because he was upset.
    b. John was frustrated after losing two games.
       Ivan is in a world of his own on Saturdays.
    c. Nathan cried three times because he was upset.
       Patricia asked a question in ceramics class.
    d. Patricia asked a question in ceramics class.
       Shirley yelled after she was hit by the ball.
    e. Shirley yelled after she was hit by the ball.
       John was frustrated after losing two games.

14. Which of the following is a sequence of overt behaviors?
    a. active, jumps, excited
    b. angry, upset, cries
    c. frustrated, depressed, anxious
    d. lazy, sleeping, tired
    e. smiles, laughs, talks

15. A participant described Marty as being "unsociable". Which
    observable behavior may have led the participant to that
    conclusion?
    a. easily distracted
    b. extremely confused
    c. does not talk
    d. often moody
    e. very inhibited

Now that you have completed the evaluation, please check your answers with the ones in the back of the book. If needed, review the material on describing behaviors and try the evaluation again. When you are satisfied with your acquisition of the information and understand your errors, turn the page and begin work on the next chapter.

CHAPTER THREE

OBSERVING BEHAVIORS

Accurate observation of behavior is essential for the application of behavior modification strategies. Effective observation is necessary to assess the quantity and extent of the behavior exhibited by the program participants. Observation cannot begin until the target behaviors are clearly described.

When the target behaviors have been accurately described, observation may proceed. This requires a clear determination of the method of observation to be utilized. Although there are many acceptable ways to observe and record behavior, the four most common methods will be considered at this time. These four recording methods are: (a) frequency (tally), (b) duration, (c) interval, and (d) instantaneous time sampling.

Frequency recording involves counting and recording each occurrence of a behavior within a given time frame. It is primarily used when the identified behavior occurs at a LOW RATE and lasts for BRIEF periods of time. Frequency recording is a particularly appropriate method of observing behavior when the target behavior has an easily defined beginning and ending. Behaviors of this nature are termed DISCRETE and they involve no uncertainty as to when they begin and end. This makes frequency recording an easily accomplished task for the observer. When a goal is to increase or decrease the number of times a behavior occurs, frequency recording is the appropriate method of observation.

FREQUENCY (TALLY) RECORDING METHOD

1 2 3 4 5 6

For instance, a child in a pre-school play program may frequently engage in the inappropriate behavior of throwing the toys against a wall. Throwing a toy against a wall is a discrete behavior that is readily observed. If the first step in modifying the behavior is to assess how often it occurs, frequency recording would be an appropriate observation method to employ. The child could be observed during a specified time period for as many days or sessions deemed necessary. Observation would simply require tallying the number of times the child threw a toy against a wall during the specified time period.

Further analysis can occur when using the frequency count. The observer can note the number of occurrences of a particular behavior during a specified amount of time and determine the *rate* of the behavior. For instance, a coach may count the number of times a basketball player makes a lay-up in one minute. Another option, using the frequency method, is to calculate the percentage or accuracy of an individual's performance. *Percentage* involves dividing the number of times the behavior occurs by the number of trials available to the individual. A person playing a card game may correctly follow directions eight out of ten times, resulting in a score of 80 percent.

Guidelines for the application of frequency recording:

1. Use with behaviors that occur at a LOW RATE and last for a BRIEF DURATION.
2. Use when behaviors are DISCRETE.
3. Use when the goal is to increase or decrease the NUMBER OF TIMES the behavior occurs.

A second method that is commonly utilized in observing behaviors is duration recording. *Duration recording* involves recording the length of time the target behavior occurs during an observation period. When using duration recording, the key consideration is how long the behavior lasts, rather than the number of times the behavior occurred. Duration recording is employed when the behavior occurs at a LOW FREQUENCY and lasts for an extended time period. The observer needs only to have a stopwatch or some other timing device to accurately record the duration of a behavior. However, duration recording does require that the behavior under observation have definite starting and ending points (a discrete behavior). When a goal of a behavior modification program is to increase or decrease the length of time a behavior occurs, duration recording is the appropriate method of observation. It may also be used when a goal is to eliminate a behavior.

DURATION RECORDING METHOD

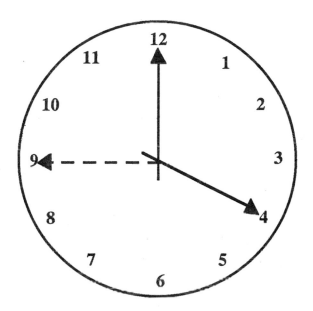

By way of illustration, a therapeutic recreation specialist may be interested in increasing the amount of time a child spends in cooperative play with other children. Before initiating efforts aimed at increasing cooperative play behavior, it is necessary to have some knowledge of how much time is currently expended by the child in the activity. During the observation periods, the therapeutic recreation specialist would need only to use a timing device to measure and record the length of time the child engaged in cooperative play with others. Intervention strategies to increase the length of time could then be determined and implemented.

Guidelines for the application of duration recording:

1. Use when behavior occurs at a LOW FREQUENCY and lasts for an EXTENDED time period.
2. Use when behavior is DISCRETE.
3. Use this procedure when the goal is to increase or decrease the LENGTH OF TIME of the occurrence.

Interval recording is the third common method of behavior observation. *Interval recording* requires that a block of time be divided into short SEGMENTS of equal length. The intervals should be short enough to allow the recording of separate occurrences of behavior but long enough to facilitate accurate observation. For instance, a 30-minute block of time could be divided into intervals of 15 seconds each. The participant is OBSERVED during each of the intervals and the target behavior RECORDED if it occurs at any time during an interval. It makes no difference if the behavior occurs once or several times during an interval; it simply is recorded as having occurred. If the behavior lasts over several intervals, it is recorded in each of the intervals that it occurs.

INTERVAL RECORDING METHOD

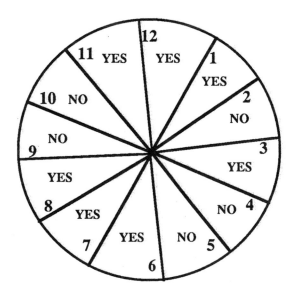

As an example, a therapeutic recreation specialist may be engaged in teaching a small group of adults with mental illness to play some simple table games at a day care center. One of the adults may be disruptive by frequently kicking a table leg. An observer might elect to divide a 30-minute period of the table game session into intervals of 15 seconds each. If the kicking behavior occurs once during a 15-second interval, the observer records the incident by making a tally for that interval. If the person kicks the table leg several times during a 15-second interval, the observer still makes only one tally for that interval. If the person kicks the table leg for 45 consecutive seconds, the observer would still simply record a single tally for each of the intervals during which the kicking occurred.

Guidelines for the application of interval recording:

1. SEGMENT observation period into short intervals.
2. OBSERVE during the pre-determined intervals.
3. RECORD if the target behavior occurred during an interval.

Instantaneous time sampling is the fourth common method of behavior observation. With *instantaneous time sampling,* behaviors are also recorded as occurring or not occurring during intervals when the participant is being observed. However, the time period does not have to be divided into shorter segments of equal length and the observer only examines the behavior at the END of the interval. The observation intervals must be of equal length but they can be separated by larger blocks of time. This technique of behavior observation is appropriate when the target behavior occurs at a high frequency and the observer does not have the time to continuously observe the clients or participants.

INSTANTANEOUS TIME SAMPLING RECORDING METHOD

To illustrate, during the evening television-viewing period in a long-term psychiatric care institution, a resident, seated on a sofa, is noticed as frequently rocking his body back and forth. A member of the evening staff is asked to observe the frequency of this behavior but does not have the time to devote to uninterrupted observation because she must also attend to other duties. The evening staff member may decide to observe the resident for a five-second interval at the end of every ten-minute period. A tally for the rocking behavior is made if it is observed during the five-second observation interval. This strategy allows the evening staff member to attend to her other duties and still make recordings of the target behavior.

When using instantaneous time sampling recording:

1. Segment observation period into INTERVALS.
2. Observe at the END of an interval and record if the target behavior occurred during the momentary observation.

Following is a list of behaviors with corresponding frequency, duration and observation information. Write the most appropriate observation method for each behavior on the line provided.

1. Arthur hits his head with his hand at a frequency of 934 per day; each hit lasts approximately one second. He may hit his head rapidly several times in succession and then refrain from such behavior for several minutes. It is difficult to determine precisely when the behavior starts or stops. _____

2. Cindy fails to attend the swimming program. The therapeutic recreation specialist would like to submit a report to her social worker about her absences. _____

3. Linda puts toys in her mouth on an average of once per hour. Each time this inappropriate behavior occurs, it lasts for five seconds. _____

4. Robert engages in conversation two times for approximately five minutes within an hour-discussion period. Because of the nature of the program, it is difficult for the recreation leader to constantly observe Robert's behavior. _____

5. Kathy practices walking three times per day. Currently she is walking an average of seven minutes per walk. _____

6. Sarah remains at the sculpting table on an average of twice per class for approximately four minutes each time she is at the table. The therapeutic recreation specialist is unable to continuously observe at her station. _____

7. During a free play period, Matthew screams loudly three times. Each outburst lasts approximately 14 minutes. _____

8. While playing basketball, Sophia uses offensive language many times (100) during a game. _____

FREQUENCY recording should be used for situations 2 and 3. Each of these behaviors occurs at a relatively low frequency and each has readily identifiable starting and ending points. In addition, the behavior described in situation 3 is of a short duration and the behavior described in situation 2 simply occurs or does not occur. These factors combine to make frequency recording the most appropriate observation method to use in both instances. The goal of a behavior modification program would be to increase the number of times Cindy attends the swimming program and to decrease the number of times Linda puts toys in her mouth.

DURATION recording should be used for situations 5 and 7. Each of these behaviors occurs at a low frequency and lasts a considerable length of time. Both behaviors also have definite starting and ending points, thus lending themselves to duration recording with a minimum of difficulty. The goal of a behavior modification program would be to increase the length of time Kathy spends in walking and to decrease the amount of time Matthew spends in screaming.

INTERVAL recording would be the appropriate observation method to use in situations 1 and 8. Both behaviors occur at a high rate of frequency and both can be recorded as having occurred or not occurred during specified time intervals. The behavior described in situation 1 might be difficult to observe for an entire day but would be easily observed for a single block of time, such as a 30-or 60-minute period divided into a series of short, equal segments. The behavior described in situation 8 would be more easily observed and recorded by intervals. The goal of a behavior modification program in each of these situations would be to reduce the number of times the inappropriate behavior occurred.

INSTANTANEOUS TIME SAMPLING should be used in situations 4 and 6. The decision to use instantaneous time sampling is based
primarily on the availability (or the lack thereof) of the observer. In circumstances such as those described in these two situations, the observer would have little latitude in choosing a method of observation. Instantaneous time sampling would allow the observer to attend to other duties and still make some observation of behaviors. The goal of a behavior modification program would probably be to increase the amount of time Robert engages in conversation and Sarah spends at the sculpting table.

When you have completed this exercise, please go to the next page and evaluate the degree to which you understand the information on methods of observing behaviors.

TEST YOUR KNOWLEDGE OF *OBSERVING BEHAVIORS*

Directions : Please circle the letter corresponding to the best
answer.

1. You are interested in determining how long Darlene engages in
   toy play. Which type of observation schedule will be used?
   a. duration
   b. frequency
   c. interval
   d. percentage
   e. time sampling

2. Jane uses an excessive amount of inappropriate verbalizations
   (average: 10 per minute) during leisure education class. Because
   of the high number of inappropriate verbalizations, what is the
   best observation schedule to use?
   a. duration
   b. frequency
   c. interval
   d. ratio
   e. time sampling

3. Which of the following would be best observed during a
   frequency count?
   a. biting (frequency: 10/week, duration: 1 second)
   b. grabbing (frequency: 4/day, duration: 2 minutes)
   c. rocking (frequency: 20/minute, duration: 2 seconds)
   d. screaming (frequency: 1/month, duration: 3 hours)
   e. spitting (frequency: 90/day, duration: 1 second)

4. Donna rarely engages in social interaction with other
   participants in the crafts program (average: once per one hour
   session). You are interested in the number of times she initiates
   interaction. Because of the low number of interactions she
   engages in, what observation schedule should you decide to use?
   a. duration
   b. frequency
   c. interval
   d. percentage
   e. time sampling

5. When wanting to increase or decrease the time a behavior lasts, which measurement method is best to use?
   a. duration recording
   b. frequency recording
   c. interval recording
   d. ratio recording
   e. time sampling recording

6. When is it best to use a frequency count?
   a. high frequency and high duration
   b. low frequency and high duration
   c. low frequency and low duration
   d. medium frequency and low duration
   e. low frequency and medium duration

7. While participating in tumbling, Jill often sits on the floor, screams, cries, and hits her knees with her hands for long periods of time. First, your objective is to decrease the time of the incident, therefore you would observe the behavior in relation to its:
   a. duration
   b. frequency
   c. interval
   d. occurrence
   e. ratio

8. Which behavior would best be observed using instantaneous time sampling?
   a. biting (frequency: 3/week, duration: 1 second)
   b. grabbing (frequency: 4/day, duration: 2 minutes)
   c. hitting (frequency: 10/day, duration: 2 seconds)
   d. screaming (frequency: 1/month, duration: 3 hours)
   e. spitting (frequency: 90/day, duration: 1 second)

9. When Steven arrives at the soccer field, he often climbs a tree and sits on a limb for long periods of time. Initially, you want to decrease the time of the incident, therefore you would observe the behavior in relationship to its:
   a. duration
   b. frequency
   c. interval
   d. occurrence
   e. ratio

10. Ben initiates conversation at a low rate and low duration while playing on the playground. You would like to increase the number of times the behavior occurs. Which observation method would be best to use?
    a. duration
    b. frequency
    c. interval
    d. ratio
    e. sampling

11. Discrete behaviors are behaviors that:
    a. are deemed to be socially acceptable.
    b. are difficult to measure because they do not have definite beginning and ending points.
    c. have been identified as being in need of modification.
    d. have definite beginning and ending points.
    e. may only be observed by use of instantaneous time sampling.

12. Accurate observation of behavior must be preceded by:
    a. measures that will insure the anonymity of the observer.
    b. precise identification of a target behavior.
    c. pre-determination of an intervention strategy.
    d. procedures that will prevent the program participant from knowing that he/she is being observed.
    e. selection of an observation method.

13. Which of the following is not an appropriate guideline for the application of frequency recording?
    a. Use when the goal is to increase the number of times the behavior occurs.
    b. Use when the behavior lasts for an extended period of time.
    c. Use when the behavior lasts for a short period of time.
    d. Use with behaviors that are discrete.
    e. Use with behaviors that occur at a low rate.

14. Which of the following is not an appropriate guideline for the application of duration recording?
    a. Use when the behavior is discrete.
    b. Use when the behavior lasts for an extended period of time.
    c. Use when the behavior occurs at a low frequency.
    d. Use when the goal is to increase the length of time the behavior occurs.
    e. Use when the goal is to increase the number of times the behavior occurs.

15. Instantaneous time sampling recording is appropriate for use when the:
    a. observation period cannot be divided into intervals.
    b. observer does not have the time to continuously observe the program participant.
    c. target behavior lasts for a short period of time.
    d. target behavior occurs at a low frequency.
    e. use of a time device is not required.

   After completing the evaluation on observing behaviors, please check your answers with the ones listed in the back of the book. If you did not perform as well as you would like, try reviewing the material in this section and give the evaluation another try. When you are satisfied with your retention of the information, please turn the page and begin work on the next chapter.

CHAPTER FOUR

MEASURING BEHAVIORS

In the course of a behavior modification program, when target
behaviors are being described, observed, and recorded, a considerable
amount of data is generated. To be useful these data must be displayed
in an efficient and clearly understood manner. The picture obtained
from this display may be developed by means of a graph. A *graph* is a
diagram that depicts the interrelationship between the program or
treatment and the behaviors of the participants. The major advantage
of a graph is its ability to quickly convey the status of a target
behavior or the effectiveness of intervention or treatment strategies. It
can provide a clear understanding of the past status of target behaviors.
The graph also has potential for use as a predictor for target behavior
change. A graph may be the most readily utilized tool available for
representation of the data systematically gathered in a leisure program.

A graph involves a vertical line and a horizontal line that
are connected to form an "L" shaped figure. The vertical line may
be referred to as the ordinate axis; the horizontal line is referred to as
the abscissa axis. The *ordinate* of a graph depicts the behavior or the
method of measurement used to observe the behavior. The *abscissa*
represents the length or periods of time during which the behavior was
observed. The ordinate and abscissa of a graph are subdivided into
uniform units of measurement and time, respectively.

The common methods of behavior measurement represented on the
ordinate of a graph include (a) frequency, (b) duration, (c) percentage
and (d) rate. Each of these measurements is appropriate for use in
specific situations.

When desiring to illustrate how often a particular behavior
occurs during a given period of time, the ordinate would be
labeled to depict *frequency*. For example, if a therapeutic
recreation specialist wished to depict how often a woman
voluntarily participated in discussions during daily leisure
education sessions over a specified period of time, a graph might
be labeled as follows:

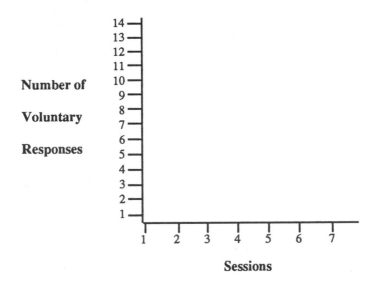

When the intent is to show how long a behavior lasts during specified time periods, the ordinate would be labeled to depict *duration*. For example, if a therapeutic recreation specialist wished to show the length of time a child remained seated during 30-minute story-telling sessions, a graph might be labeled as follows:

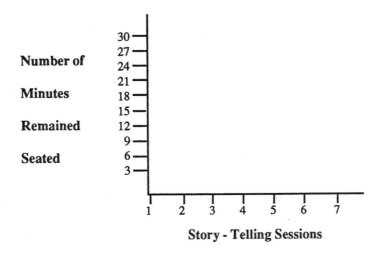

A graph may also be used to depict the *percentages* of time particular behaviors occur or any other factors that lend themselves to expression by percentages. For example, a boy in a day camp program requires the use of the restroom facilities several times during the morning sessions but often refuses to wash his hands after toileting. A graph that illustrates the percentage of time he engaged in the desired behavior of hand washing could be labeled as follows:

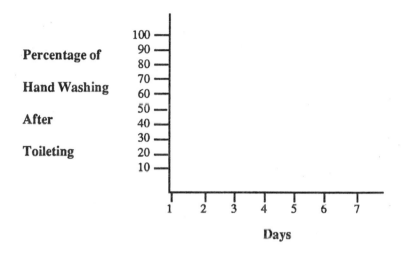

A graph may also be used to illustrate the *rate* of a particular behavior. In so doing, the ordinate of a graph would contain units representing the number of responses (behaviors) divided by the length of time required to elicit those responses. For example, a man in a therapeutic exercise class may be given several one-minute trials to see how many basketball lay-ups he can make. A graph that depicts his rate of success for this particular basketball shot could be labeled as follows:

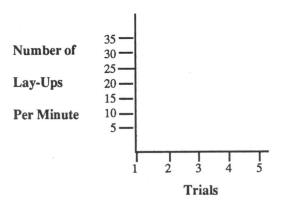

The common measurements represented on the ordinate of a graph include:

1. Frequency
2. Duration
3. Percentage
4. Rate

The abscissa of a graph always represents the units of time that were utilized to observe and measure the behavior represented on the ordinate. The abscissa could include such units of time as minutes, hours, days, weeks, or months. It could also include units representing time periods such as classes, sessions, trials, etc.

Follow these directions to successfully graph the occurrences of a behavior:

1. After the unit of time (on the abscissa) has passed, go up the ordinate until you come to the number corresponding to the behavior's occurrence.
2. Move directly across to the right of that number until you come to the place above the number on the abscissa that corresponds with the time the observation was made, and make a dot.

3. Plot the graph by starting with the dot that represents the first observation. Draw a straight line between it and the dot that represents the second observation. Connect the second dot to the third dot and proceed in this fashion until all the dots are connected.

On the graph located below, graph the following data, following the previous instructions.

Day 1. Frequency 24.
Day 2. Frequency 26.
Day 3. Frequency 16.
Day 4. Frequency 12.
Day 5. Frequency 18.
Day 6. Frequency 10.
Day 7. Frequency 4.
Day 8. Frequency 6.
Day 9. Frequency 2.
Day 10. Frequency 0.

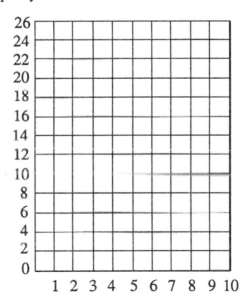

When you have completed graphing the ten days, please turn to the next page.

If your graph looks like the one on the following page, you have the right idea!

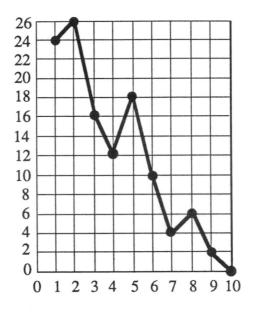

Prior to the initiation of an intervention strategy, an observation period occurs. This observation period is termed a *baseline*. During a baseline, no attempt is made to change or influence the behavior, except perhaps to set the occasion for the behavior to occur. The length of time taken for the baseline varies according to the severity of the behavior. Baseline observation on a graph is set aside from the remainder of the graph by a vertical dotted line, drawn between the last baseline observation and the first treatment observation. The baseline period is the pre-treatment record which allows comparison with data from the intervention phases later in the program.

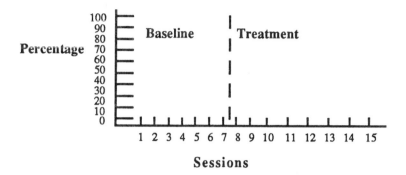

Sessions

Once the data have been plotted on the graph, there are three different interpretations which can be made from the information.

1. If the general slope of the line is upward, the behavior is increasing. This movement is termed *acceleration*.

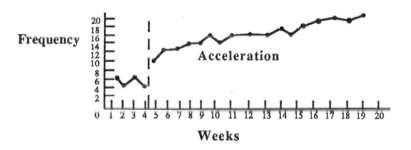

Weeks

2. If the general slope of the line is downward, the behavior is decreasing. This movement is termed *deceleration*.

35

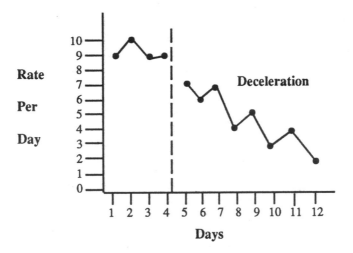

3. If the slope of the line is parallel with the horizontal line, the behavior is neither increasing nor decreasing. The behavior is said to be *maintained*.

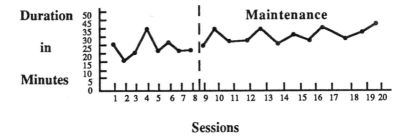

Three possible interpretations of data plotted on a graph:

1. Acceleration
2. Deceleration
3. Maintenance

You have now completed the information on graphing. Please go to the next page and evaluate how well you retained the material.

36

TEST YOUR KNOWLEDGE OF *MEASURING BEHAVIORS*

Directions: Please circle the letter corresponding to the best answer.

1. When measuring the duration of a behavior, what units are represented on the ordinate of a graph?
   a. how often the behavior occurs
   b. the accuracy of performance
   c. the extent to which the behavior returns
   d. the length of time a behavior occurs
   e. the number of responses divided by the time required

2. Prior to the initiation of an intervention strategy, Debbie was observed for a week. Her daily rate of crying was 27 during this time period. Intervention began at the start of the second week and her daily rate dropped to 10. During the third week it reached a daily rate of 38. A revision in the strategy was made during the fourth week and the daily rate dropped to 20. What was Debbie's average daily rate of crying during baseline?
   a. 38
   b. 27
   c. 20
   d. 10
   e. 0

3. When measuring the rate of behavior, what units are represented on the ordinate of a graph?
   a. how often the behavior occurs
   b. the accuracy of the performance
   c. the extent to which the behavior returns
   d. the length of time a behavior occurs
   e. the number of responses divided by the time required

4. What is the term used to describe the observation period prior to the initiation of an intervention strategy?
   a. baseline
   b. deprivation
   c. duration
   d. acceleration
   e. maintenance

5. When measuring the frequency of the behavior, what units are represented on the ordinate of a graph?
   a. how often the behavior occurs
   b. the accuracy of performance
   c. the extent to which the behavior returns
   d. the length of time the behavior occurs
   e. the number of responses divided by the time required

6. What does the abscissa represent on a graph?
   a. numbers
   b. percentage
   c. rate
   d. space
   e. time

7. When measuring the percentage of the behavior, what units are represented on the ordinate of a graph?
   a. how often the behavior returns
   b. the accuracy of the performance
   c. the extent to which the behavior returned
   d. the length of time a behavior occurs
   e. the number of responses divided by the time required

8. What are the possible units of measurement included on the ordinate?
   a. minutes, days, weeks, months
   b. duration, percentage, rate, frequency
   c. frequency, interval, ratio, percentage
   d. rate, duration, minutes, weeks
   e. ratio, interval, time sampling, rate

9. What is the term used to describe the behavior that is pictured by the slope of the line pointing downward on a graph?
   a. accelerating
   b. being maintained
   c. decelerating
   d. negatively reinforced
   e. positively reinforced

10. When the slope of the line on a graph is pointing upward, the behavior is:
    a. accelerating
    b. being extinguished
    c. being maintained
    d. being punished
    e. decelerating

11. A graph is a diagram that depicts the relationship between:
    a. rate and duration.
    b. the observer and the program participant.
    c. the ordinate and the rate of behavior.
    d. the target behavior and the terminal behavior.
    e. two variables.

12. A major advantage of a graph is its ability to
    a. describe the target behavior.
    b. predict baseline data.
    c. quickly indicate the relationship between the observer and the program participant.
    d. quickly indicate the status of the target behavior.
    e. select an intervention strategy.

13. On a graph, baseline data and treatment data are separated by:
    a. a two-week time period.
    b. a horizontal dotted line.
    c. a vertical dotted line.
    d. a vertical solid line.
    e. the ordinate.

14. The length of time required for gathering baseline data depends on the:
    a. complexity of the treatment strategy.
    b. cooperation of the observed.
    c. length of the treatment time.
    d. severity of the target behavior.
    e. skill of the observer.

15. When the line on a graph is generally parallel to the abscissa, the behavior is:
    a. accelerating.
    b. being extinguished.
    c. being maintained.
    d. being punished.
    e. decelerating.

Now that you have completed the evaluation, please check your answers with the ones listed in the back of the book. When you are satisfied with your retention of the information, you are ready to begin work on the next chapter.

CHAPTER FIVE

UNDERSTANDING BEHAVIORS: SEQUENCE ANALYSIS

The basis of the behavior modification approach is the belief that behavior is primarily influenced by environmental agents. Behavior is learned; it is not inherent. If behavior is learned, it is capable of alteration or modification by additional learning. The goal of a behavior modification program is to alter the target behavior. However, that is not possible if the program focuses on the target behavior only, as if it were an isolated event, independent of environmental conditions and influences. Attempting to modify behavior without benefit of any knowledge related to environmental conditions is difficult. Recognition and understanding of environmental events that influence the target behavior is extremely helpful. Because manipulation of environmental events is a fundamental aspect of behavior modification, knowledge of which events or conditions to manipulate is necessary for success. Thus, assessment of events that occur prior to and following the target behavior is as important as accurate description and observation of the target behavior itself.

Those events that occur PRIOR to the target behavior, and in some way influence the behavior, are termed *antecedent* conditions. These conditions could include such factors as where the antecedent events occurred, when they occurred, who was present at their occurrence, and what activities and incidents transpired before the target behavior occurred. If the antecedent conditions or events are capable of manipulation, then the potential exists for the modification of the target behavior. For example, if the inappropriate behavior of hitting others is demonstrated by a participant while playing softball, it may be useful for the therapeutic recreation specialist to identify possible antecedent conditions. Upon examination, the specialist observes that the participant begins to hit others after another player calls her names. To PREVENT this participant from hitting other players the specialist may take the following two actions: (a) tell the player doing the hitting prior to each game that the first time the other player calls her a name to immediately inform the specialist, and (b) speak with the player calling names and explain the ramifications of his actions. Conversely,

41

another player is observed who does not smile during the entire softball game. The therapeutic recreation specialist observes him closely during a game and observes he frequently fails when batting (striking out) and when fielding (dropping the ball). To ENCOURAGE smiling during softball the specialist establishes practice sessions to enhance the person's softball skills.

Characteristics of antecedents:

1. Occur PRIOR to the target behavior.
2. PREVENT or ENCOURAGE behaviors.

Those events that occur AFTER the target behavior has been exhibited, and in some way are influenced by or related to the behavior, are termed *consequences*. It is important to determine the precise relationship between a consequence and the target behavior. The behavior can be modified only if the consequence follows each occurrence of the target behavior and is not present at other times; that is, it is not independent of the target behavior. If the consequence does not consistently follow the target behavior, manipulation of the consequence will not result in any orderly modification of the target behavior.

If a consequence consistently follows the occurrence of the target behavior and if it is not otherwise present, it is said to be *contingent*. Contingent consequences lend themselves to manipulation and, thus, to the modification of the target behavior. For example, if successfully defining *leisure* in a leisure education class is followed by the pleasant consequence of a wink, then insuring the presence of the consequence will ENCOURAGE the future occurrence of the behavior. Conversely, if talking out of turn is followed by an unpleasant consequence such as a recreation professional ignoring the person, then insuring the presence of the consequence will DISCOURAGE the future occurrence of the behavior.

Characteristics of consequences:

1. Occur AFTER the target behavior.
2. ENCOURAGE or DISCOURAGE likelihood of future behaviors.

SEQUENCE ANALYSIS

ANTECEDENT   **BEHAVIOR**   **CONSEQUENCE**

Following is an exercise related to antecedents, behaviors, and consequences. Please follow the directions.

After the recreation resource session was over, the participants were required to return the recreation equipment they used to its original location. When the time came to return the equipment, Gloria pounded her fists on the ground, kicked her toys, and screamed. The leader of the recreation resource session would calm her down by singing her a song. Gloria's crying and screaming would eventually stop.

1. What was Gloria's behavior and the antecedent and consequence of the behavior?
   ANTECEDENT: _____ .
   BEHAVIOR: _____ .
   CONSEQUENCE: _____ .
2. What was the therapeutic recreation leader's behavior and the antecedent and consequence of the behavior?
   ANTECEDENT: _____ .
   BEHAVIOR: _____ .
   CONSEQUENCE: _____ .

If your answer looks like the following, you're doing fine.

1. ANTECEDENT: *The recreation resource session ended.*
   BEHAVIOR: *Gloria screamed and kicked her toys.*
   CONSEQUENCE: *The recreation leader sang to Gloria.*
2. ANTECEDENT: *Gloria screamed and kicked her toys.*
   BEHAVIOR: *The recreation leader sang to Gloria.*
   CONSEQUENCE: *Gloria's screaming stopped.*

Notice that in the example each person's behavior affected the other's. It is also important to note that the first example focused on Gloria's behavior while the second example concentrated on the behavior of the recreation leader. These examples illustrate the behavior that all people (even recreation professionals) are continuously modified by the behaviors of the people they encounter.

In summary, the antecedent occurs BEFORE a behavior and the consequence FOLLOWS the behavior. Behaviors can be prevented or encouraged by manipulation of the antecedent or consequence. The result is an increase or decrease in the likelihood of the behavior occurring in the future.

Now that you have completed the exercise on examining antecedents and consequences of behaviors, please go to the next page and evaluate your knowledge of this material.

TEST YOUR KNOWLEDGE OF SEQUENCE ANALYSIS

Directions: Please circle the letter corresponding to the best answer.

1. What is the term that describes the event that follows a behavior?
   a. antecedent
   b. behavior
   c. consequence
   d. punisher
   e. reinforcement

2. What is the word that is used to describe the event that occurs before a behavior?
   a. antecedent
   b. behavior
   c. consequence
   d. punisher
   e. reinforcement

3. What should you manipulate if you would like to prevent or encourage a behavior?
   a. antecedent
   b. behavior
   c. consequence
   d. punisher
   e. reinforcer

4. Eric was watching television when a staff member told him to go the gymnasium. While walking to the gym, William pushed Eric to the ground. After reaching the gym, Eric reported the incident to the therapeutic recreation specialist. William said he was wrong and apologized to Eric. What was the antecedent condition to Eric being pushed to the ground?
   a. being cued to go to the gym
   b. receiving an apology from William
   c. reporting the incident
   d. walking to the gym
   e. watching television

Directions: Based on the information from the following paragraph, answer the next two associated questions.

Marcie is at a picnic in the park and wanders from the group. The therapeutic recreation specialist finds her and tells her she should not leave the group and returns Marcie to the group. After a short while Marcie wanders off again. The therapeutic recreation specialist finds her and requires her to pick up trash. Marcie again wanders off. When the therapeutic recreation specialist finally finds her, Marcie is sent to the bus where she must wait until it is time to return from the picnic.

5. What was the first consequence of Marcie's problem behavior?
    a. attending a picnic in the park
    b. confined to the bus
    c. picking up trash
    d. returning home
    e. verbal reprimands

6. What was the second consequence of Marcie's problem behavior?
    a. attending a picnic in the park
    b. confined to the bus
    c. picking up trash
    d. returning home
    e. verbal reprimand

Directions: Based on the information from the following two paragraphs, answer the two associated questions.

Gerald has exhibited some aggressive behaviors after attending the first few therapeutic recreation programs. When cued to participate in activities, Gerald begins to swing his arms and kick the nearest chair. Each time he does this, the recreation leader will come over to him and coax him to the group.
Preliminary information showed that Gerald swung his arms and kicked on the average of seven times each session. A program was initiated where Gerald was reinforced with verbal praise every time he came to an activity after being told only once. If, when asked to participate in an activity, he began swinging his arms and kicking, he was required to stand in the corner for five minutes.

7. After the program was initiated, what was the antecedent of the desired behavior?
   a. coaxed by recreation leader
   b. cued to participate
   c. swinging his arms and kicking
   d. standing in the corner for five minutes
   e. reinforced with verbal praise

8. Before the program was initiated, what was the consequence of the problem behavior?
   a. Gerald came to the activity.
   b. Gerald swung his arms.
   c. Gerald was coaxed by the leader.
   d. Gerald was cued to participate.
   e. Gerald was required to stand in the corner.

Directions: Based on the information in the next paragraph, answer the three associated questions.

Philip frequently forgot about his leisure education class. He was usually reminded by his mother to attend. Often he arrived at the recreation center late and had to wait for a break in the discussion before joining the group. For his birthday, Philip's father gave him a watch. Now Philip looks at his watch and arrives on time to his class.

9. What was the antecedent to Philip going to leisure education class before he received the watch?
   a. he forgot about the class
   b. he looked at his watch
   c. he was late for class
   d. his father gave him a watch
   e. his mother reminded him to go

10. What was the consequence of him arriving late to class?
    a. he attended class
    b. he had to wait to participate
    c. he left for the recreation center
    d. his father gave him a watch
    e. his mother reminded him to go

11. What is the antecedent to Philip now arriving on time?
    a. being reminded to attend
    b. having to wait to participate
    c. forgetting to go to class
    d. looking at his watch
    e. receiving the watch

12. Behavior modification is based on the belief that:
    a. behavior is learned.
    b. behavior is primarily influenced by genetic rather than
       environmental factors.
    c. environmental agents have little influence on behavior
    d. environmental conditions should be ignored when an
       individual's behavior is assessed.
    e. individuals cannot be accountable for their own behavior.

13. A therapeutic recreation specialist can best apply behavior
    modification techniques by:
    a. concentrating on behaviors that are independent of
       environmental influences.
    b. disregarding a behavior's antecedent and accurately
       describing its consequences.
    c. disregarding environmental conditions and focusing on the
       target behavior.
    d. focusing on the target behavior and its antecedents and
       consequences.
    e. manipulating influential internal agents.

14. A contingent consequence is one that is:
    a. consistently present after the occurrence of a behavior
       and is not present at other times.
    b. consistently present prior to the occurrence of a behavior
       and is not present at other times.
    c. independent of the target behavior.
    d. intermittently present after the occurrence of a behavior.
    e. intermittently present prior to the occurrence of a
       behavior.

15. Which of the following is the sequential relationship that must be determined prior to the application of behavior modification techniques?
    a. antecedent - behavior - consequence
    b. antecedent - consequence - behavior
    c. behavior - antecedent - consequence
    d. behavior - antecedent - environmental agents
    e. environmental agents - consequence - behavior

After completing the evaluation please check your answers with those recorded in the back of the book. When you are satisfied with the knowledge you have acquired, please turn the page and begin work on the next chapter.

CHAPTER SIX

ACCELERATING BEHAVIORS: POSITIVE REINFORCEMENT

Positive reinforcement is the cornerstone of most behavior modification programs. It is regarded as one of the most crucial factors in influencing individuals to change behaviors and, thus, is also one of the most commonly applied behavior modification procedures. *Positive reinforcement* is the PRESENTATION or delivery of a consequence that makes a behavior occur MORE OFTEN in the future. As is true in other aspects of behavior modification, the behavior to be reinforced must be specific and measurable in order to assess whether change is actually occurring. It is also essential that the relationship among the target behavior, the delivered consequence, and subsequent behavior is clearly understood. Remember that the consequence that is delivered after the behavior occurs is the positive *reinforcer;* the process of delivering the consequence is positive *reinforcement.*

For example, a happy-face button is given to Sarah after she successfully draws a picture of a tree. If this is continued and Sarah begins drawing the tree more often, the button would then be identified as a positive reinforcer because:

1. The reinforcement involved the PRESENTATION of the button;
2. The behavior began occurring MORE OFTEN.

In another example, after Clarence hit Mary he was scolded. However, Clarence began hitting Mary more often. The scolding could then be interpreted as a positive reinforcer to Clarence because:

1. The reinforcement involved the PRESENTATION of scolding, and
2. The behavior began occurring MORE OFTEN.

Few people would subjectively evaluate scolding as pleasant or desirable. Typically, scolding would not intentionally be used as a positive reinforcer. Nevertheless, in this case, scolding is a positive reinforcer. An important point to remember is that it is

51

possible for a consequence to reinforce an undesired behavior.

There are two major categories of reinforcers: (a) primary and (b) secondary.

1. *Primary reinforcers* are those reinforcers that are necessary to maintain bodily functions, such as nourishment or food, air, and warmth. These reinforcers are termed *unconditioned reinforcers* because they are not learned.
2. *Secondary reinforcers,* also known as *conditioned reinforcers,* are learned. This category of reinforcers is further divided into three sub-categories.
   a. *Social reinforcers* involve interaction between two or more persons. Examples could include smiling, a wink, or words of praise.
   b. *Activity reinforcers* involve participation in an event. Examples could include playing a game, going on an outing, or taking a walk.
   c. *Token reinforcers* are objects that can be exchanged for a desirable item or activity. Token reinforcers have little value in themselves. The value of tokens lies in what can be purchased or traded for with them.

Money, credit cards, and checks, items that are used in our everyday lives, are examples of token reinforcers. These tokens are not meaningful to us because of what they are (paper and plastic), but because of what we can obtain with, or exchange for, them. Much of our leisure participation is facilitated through the use of these tokens. Tokens are often used for convenience and, in some situations, one token may be exchanged for another token. For example, when people are playing poker they are using poker chips (tokens) that are cashed in for money (tokens), which then can be used to purchase desired items.

A token system also may be used in a recreation program. For example, a therapeutic recreation specialist could place a mark beside participants' names, written on a chalkboard, who have recently completed a desired task. After receiving five marks, each individual is then allowed to participate in a desired leisure activity with a recreation volunteer. In this example, the check mark acts as a token that can be exchanged for a desired leisure activity.

Reinforcer Categories

1. Primary

Maintain body functions

2. Secondary
A. Social

Interaction between 2 or more persons

B. Activity

Participation in an event

C. Token

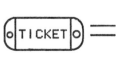 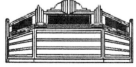

Objects exchange for desired item/activity

Various objects and events may be used as positive reinforcers. For some people many types of food and drink are positive reinforcers, while praise and attention are desired by numerous others. Reinforcers differ from one person to another. The expression "one person's junk is another person's treasure" is appropriate in this context. In every case the selection of an object or event to serve as a positive reinforcer must be person specific; that is, it must be something that will effectively influence that individual's behavior. A delivered consequence is a positive reinforcer only if it works. The question of whether the consequence would serve as a positive reinforcer for the general population is not relevant. For example, raw oysters would be a positive reinforcer for some individuals but not for others, while hot, spicy food may also be a positive reinforcer to some but not for others. Praise from the therapeutic recreation specialist may be a positive reinforcer to one participant but not for another. Remember that the actual effect the consequence has on the behavior must be considered rather than the intended effect.

The selection of a consequence to serve as a positive reinforcer for a specific individual may take some time to accomplish. It may also involve a considerable amount of trial and error before a positive reinforcer is discovered. This, sometimes lengthy, selection process should not be regarded as a discouraging factor.

Try this as an exercise. Listed below is a series of items and events that could potentially serve as reinforcers. In the space to the right of the item or event, indicate whether it could serve as a primary, social, activity, or token reinforcer.

1. a dollar bill _____

2. playing chess _____

3. drawing a picture _____

4. a handshake _____

5. an ice cream cone _____

6. a blanket _____

7. a pat on the back _____

8. going to a ball game _____

9. a pass to a stageplay   _____

10. watching television   _____

11. a candy bar   _____

12. a hug   _____

13. quiet conversation   _____

14. a library card   _____

15. listening to music   _____

16. a glass of water   _____

17. a compliment   _____

18. reading a book   _____

19. eating a hot dog   _____

20. a gift certificate   _____

If you indicated that 1, 9, 14, and 20 were token reinforcers, 2, 3, 8, 10, 15, and 18 were activity reinforcers, 4, 7, 12, 13, and 17 were social reinforcers, and 5, 6, 11, 16, and 19 were primary reinforcers, you completed the exercise correctly. The important point to remember is that there is a great diversity of items or events that can serve as positive reinforcers.

There are techniques that can be employed by the therapeutic recreation specialist to help facilitate the selection of a positive reinforcer. One such technique is known as the PREMACK PRINCIPLE. The *Premack Principle* involves the linking of the behavior to be reinforced with another behavior in which the individual likes to engage. It is based on the premise that the opportunity to engage in a preferred or favorite activity by an individual can be used to reinforce a target behavior that occurs less often than the favorite behavior. The Premack Principle requires careful OBSERVATION of an individual during times when that individual has the opportunity to choose behaviors in which to engage. The behavior that the individual spends the most time doing or does most often when a number of options are available can often be effective as a positive reinforcer. Thus, the essence of the Premack Principle is as follows: If the opportunity to engage in a HIGH FREQUENCY DURATION behavior is provided as a consequence of performing a LOW FREQUENCY DURATION behavior, the opportunity to do the high frequency behavior will act as areinforcer for the low frequency behavior. For instance, each time the recreation practitioner asks the children participating in the recreation program to choose the game they want to participate in, the children continuously choose the game Uno™ (high frequency behavior). The children choose this game because they may not know how to play the other available games or may not feel confident that they will succeed in the other games. In an attempt to expand the children's leisure repertoires, the practitioner employs the Premack Principle by stating that if the children play a leisure resource game (low frequency behavior) for the first portion of the session, then they will be able to play Uno™ (high frequency behavior) for the second portion of the session.

Guidelines for the application of the Premack Principle:

1. OBSERVATION when an individual has choice of activities.
2. Provide opportunity for a HIGH FREQUENCY DURATION behavior contingent on a LOW FREQUENCY DURATION behavior.

Utilization of positive reinforcement as a behavior modification technique requires some understanding of the principles of deprivation and satiation. A consequence that is readily available to an individual is not likely to serve as an effective positive reinforcer. In general, it is necessary for the individual to have gone without a particular conse-quence for some time prior to its delivery for it to be an effective positive reinforcer. The consequence will have little or no effect as a reinforcer of behavior if it is readily available. *Deprivation* refers to the period of time preceding a positive reinforcement session during which the individual was denied, or had no opportunity to receive, the reinforcer. *Satiation* describes the condition in which the consequence has been provided for so long or so often that it has lost its effectiveness and no longer serves as a reinforcer. As an example, a therapeutic recreation specialist working at a long term care geriatric facility decides to use refreshments such as fresh fruit and juice to entice residents to attend the evening recreation program that is conducted immediately following dinner. If the residents received as much fresh fruit and juice at dinner as they desired, they may be temporarily "satiated" with the reinforcers of fruit amd juice.

However, if these items were not available during dinner, the residents would be "deprived" of the reinforcer. This deprivation of fruit and juice at dinner may strenghten the likelihood that these items will be viewed as reinforcers by the residents.

The concept of DEPRIVATION may complicate the process of positive reinforcement. Deprivation of a primary reinforcer may be an appropriate procedure or it may be a serious issue that has legal, moral, and ethical ramifications, depending on the circumstances. Deprivation of a primary reinforcer should be thoroughly examined from all perspectives before it is employed. Deprivation of secondary reinforcers also requires careful consideration but it may not raise questions of a similar nature.

SATIATION implies that, if possible, the positive reinforcer should be provided to an individual in small amounts or for short lengths of time and that it should be alternated with other equally effective reinforcers. It also implies that the reinforcer(s) not be available to the individual outside the context of the positive reinforcement sessions. The possibility of satiation requires careful monitoring by the therapeutic recreation specialist.

Characteristics of amount of reinforcement:

1. DEPRIVATION involves withholding a reinforcer.
2. SATIATION involves the excessive use of a reinforcer so that it loses its effectiveness.

You have now completed the information on positive reinforcement. Please turn the page and evaluate how well you retained the information.

TEST YOUR KNOWLEDGE OF *POSITIVE REINFORCEMENT*

Directions: Please circle the letter corresponding to the best answer.

1. Check marks are placed on a chart whenever Molly completes an activity. When 20 check marks are earned, Molly will go on a shopping trip. The check marks serve as what type of reinforcer?
   a. activity
   b. negative
   c. primary
   d. social
   e. token

2. What is the term used to describe the temporary withholding of a reinforcer to make it more effective?
   a. contingency contracting
   b. deprivation
   c. Premack Principle
   d. punishment
   e. satiation

3. What is an example of a primary reinforcer?
   a. eating a carrot
   b. getting a trophy
   c. going to the library
   d. receiving a dollar
   e. saying "very good"

4. What is the best example of the Premack Principle?
   a. if you eat ice cream now, you must eat dinner tonight.
   b. if you go to the movies this morning, you must take out the trash this afternoon.
   c. if you mop the floor now, you may go to the movies tonight.
   d. if you spill the water at lunch, you have to mop the floor after eating.
   e. if you take out the trash today, you may mop the floor tomorrow.

5. Barbara has participated appropriately in all groups for the day and you reinforce her with a token. Which reinforcer might you use?
   a. a trip to the library
   b. one cookie
   c. saying "excellent participation"
   d. two dollars
   e. verbal praise

6. What is an example of an activity reinforcer?
   a. eating an apple
   b. getting a blue ribbon
   c. going to the museum
   d. receiving a quarter
   e. saying "nice coloring"

7. Jason will go outside and hit the tether ball every chance he gets. You decide to use this activity as a reinforcer and let Jason go outside for 5 minutes every time he completes a scheduled program. By the end of the day Jason has tired. After his evening program you allow him to go outside again. Instead of going outside, Jason frowns and walks to his bedroom. In reference to hitting the tetherball, what has Jason become?
   a. confused
   b. deprived
   c. generalized
   d. reinforced
   e. satiated

8. Two behaviors are identified, one of which occurs more frequently than the other. What is the term used to describe the principle that makes the opportunity to engage in the high frequency behavior contingent upon the occurrence of the low frequency behavior?
   a. contingency contracting
   b. deprivation
   c. punishment
   d. satiation
   e. the Premack Principle

9. A consequence is not a positive reinforcer unless it follows the behavior and the behavior:
   a. decreases
   b. increases
   c. is deprived
   d. is satiated
   e. remains the same

10. Greg has completed all his programs for the day and you socially reinforce him. Which of the following is considered a social reinforcer?
    a. drinking coffee
    b. going to the library
    c. playing cards
    d. receiving praise
    e. receiving 50 cents

11. What is the term used to describe the temporary or permanent loss of an item's reinforcing properties due to it being offered too often or in too great a quantity?
    a. contingency contracting
    b. deprivation
    c. Premack Principle
    d. punishment
    e. satiation

12. What is an example of a social reinforcer?
    a. eating an ice cream cone
    b. getting a trophy
    c. going to the library
    d. receiving a dollar
    e. saying "that's nice sharing"

13. What is the most desirable consequence when working with participants?
    a. deprivation
    b. extinction
    c. positive reinforcement
    d. punishment
    e. satiation

14. Positive reinforcement is the presentation of a consequence that:
    a. changes a high frequency behavior to a low frequency behavior.
    b. eliminates an inappropriate behavior.
    c. is dependent on neither primary nor secondary reinforcers.
    d. is unconditioned.
    e. make a behavior occur more often in the future.

15. Secondary reinforcers are:
    a. conditioned.
    b. contingent.
    c. inherent.
    d. less effective.
    e. unconditioned.

When you complete the evaluation, please turn to the back of the book and compare your answers to the ones provided. When you are satisfied with your retention of the information, please begin work on the next chapter.

CHAPTER SEVEN

ACCELERATING BEHAVIORS: NEGATIVE REINFORCEMENT

Any consideration of the concept of reinforcement of behavior is not complete without giving some attention to the topic of negative reinforcement. As with positive reinforcement, negative reinforcement is a method that will increase the strength of a behavior. It increases the strength of a behavior by removing or postponing an AVERSIVE antecedent, CONTINGENT on the occurrence of the behavior. An aversive antecedent refers to some ongoing object, event, or stimulus that is present in the environment and is not desired by the individual whose behavior is to be reinforced. It is necessary for an aversive condition to exist, or have the possibility of existing, in the environment in order for negative reinforcement to be effective. When the individual engages in the appropriate behavior, the aversive condition is removed. The consequence of the behavior is avoidance of, or escape from, the ongoing aversive condition.

Characteristics of negative reinforcement:

1. Removal or postponement of an AVERSIVE antecedent.
2. Removal or postponement is CONTINGENT on a target behavior.

Any object, event, stimulus, or condition that increases the frequency or duration of a behavior is reinforcement for that behavior. The reinforcement is positive if it involves the delivery or presentation of a consequence that is desired by the participant, after the participant has engaged in the appropriate behavior. In other words, something that is desired by the individual has been added to the situation. Reinforcement is negative if it involves the elimination or postponement of something from the environment that is aversive to the participant, after the participant has engaged in the appropriate behavior. In other words, something that is not desired by the participant has been removed from the situation. In either case, the behavior of the individual is strengthened.

Some general characteristics that apply to positive reinforcement are also applicable to negative reinforcement. The removal of an aversive condition that serves as a negative reinforcer for one individual may not serve as a negative reinforcer for others. In addition, a condition may be perceived as being aversive for an individual at one time but not at other times. The removal of an aversive condition is a negative reinforcer only if it strengthens behavior. Negative reinforcement must be evaluated in terms of its actual effect on the individual, not on its anticipated effect.

There are two major procedures involved in negative reinforcement. The first is known as the ESCAPE procedure. In the case of *escape,* the aversive antecedent is presented to the individual. When the person responds by engaging in the appropriate behavior, the antecedent is immediately removed. Many individuals use escape procedures in the normal course of events. For instance, an individual with a toothache may take aspirin to alleviate the pain. The individual will be more likely to take aspirin in the future because it removed the aversive event of the toothache. The individual escaped from the pain of the toothache. Similarly, a young girl in a recreation program may scream. Screaming is an unpleasant sound to the recreation leader. A response by the leader that removes the screaming, such as yelling at the girl, will tend to recur when the girl screams again. The leader's response of yelling at the participant is strengthened by turning off (escaping from) the girl's screaming. The leader's behavior of yelling will be more likely to be repeated when a participant screams in the future.

In summary, the escape procedure involves the removal of an aversive antecedent, contingent on a behavior. This procedure then increases the strength of the behavior.

The second major procedure in negative reinforcement is called the AVOIDANCE procedure. With the *avoidance* procedure an individual prevents the potential aversive condition from occurring by engaging in appropriate behavior. If the behavior occurs, the aversive antecedent is not presented. Thus, the behavior is strengthened. If the behavior is not performed, the negative reinforcer is presented.

Avoidance procedures also operate frequently in people's everyday routines. For instance, individuals pay their bills regularly to avoid repossession of material goods or loss of utilities, such as water and electricity. The bill-paying behavior is negatively reinforced by the desire to avoid unpleasant consequences. Adherence to posted speed limits is often negatively reinforced by avoidance of receiving speeding tickets. If a man participating in a recreation program knocks over some equipment, he may leave the activity room to avoid having to re-position the equipment. His avoidance of the therapeutic recreation specialist negatively reinforces his behavior of running away.

In summary, the avoidance procedure involves the prevention or postponement of an aversive condition, contingent on a behavior. This procedure then increases the strength of the behavior.

Try this as an exercise to achieve a greater understanding of escape and avoidance. Following are ten examples of negative reinforcement. On the line following each example write "escape" if that is the procedure that is in operation; if avoidance is the procedure in operation, write "avoidance" on the line. Keep in mind that program leaders and program participants alike can have behaviors that are strengthened by negative reinforcement.

1. At the conclusion of the arts and crafts session, the instructor detains each participant until his or her individual work area is cleaned up and all materials and tools are properly stored. When each work area passes the instructor's inspection, the individual program participant is allowed to leave and prepare for the next activity.

_____

2. At summer camp, Bobby learns that counselors and other camp staff are empowered with the right to issue demerits as a form of discipline. During cabin inspection, an unmade bed can result in three demerits for a guilty camper. After arising, the first thing Bobby does is make his bed.

_____

3. During dance class the instructor observes when Glen and Carol are paired, they do not try to learn the dance steps. Instead they spend their time deliberately bumping into the other dancers. This annoys the instructor. In future class sessions the instructor uses pairing techniques that prevent Glen and Carol being partners.

_____

65

4. In preparing for the community theater presentation, the director requires the cast to know their lines perfectly. During rehearsals, the cast must repeat a scene until they do it without making any mistakes before she will allow them to take a break.

_____

5. When the music therapy sessions near their end, the leader allows the participants to devote the final 10 minutes to any type of music they wish to hear. Because she does not like country/western music, whenever that type of music is chosen the leader ends the session a few minutes earlier than scheduled and tinkers with the equipment.

_____

6. During the first day of softball practice the coach announces that, in the future, anyone who is late will be required to run five laps around the field when practice is over. Eddie makes sure that he always gets to practice on time.

_____

7. When Mark signs up to go on an afternoon canoe outing, he is told that anyone on the outing who is caught littering will not be allowed to go on a subsequent two-day canoe trip. Mark is careful not to litter on the outing.

_____

8. The recreation therapist is teaching Ellen to play checkers. In the initial session Ellen popped her gum constantly until the therapist asked her to remove it. Now when Ellen begins to pop her gum, the therapist immediately asks her to remove it from her mouth and put it in the wastebasket.

_____

9. During the drop-in period at a local recreation center, children are allowed to play any games that are available. When older boys are present Virginia is afraid to play table tennis because she is afraid they will make fun of her lack of playing skills. She waits until the boys leave before she tries to play.

_____

10. On the first morning of a backpacking trip, the leader misreads a map and the group becomes lost. The group grumbles about not knowing where they are. It is mid-afternoon before they find familiar landmarks. On subsequent days the leader carefully examines the map before beginning the day's hike.

_____

If you indicated that 1, 4, 5, and 8 are examples of the escape procedure and 2, 3, 6, 7, 9, and 10 were examples of the avoidance procedure, you did the exercise correctly.

The two major procedures associated with negative reinforcement:

1. ESCAPE
2. AVOIDANCE

Because negative reinforcement requires the presence, or the threat, of an aversive condition, it should generally be regarded as an extreme measure and used as a last resort. Negative reinforcement should not be employed if the same objectives can be achieved by the use of positive reinforcement. It is unlikely that a complex negative reinforcement strategy would be employed outside a clinical setting, with a carefully controlled procedure monitored by a group of behavioral experts.

To evaluate your retention of the material presented on negative reinforcement, go to the next page and complete the exercise.

TEST YOUR KNOWLEDGE OF *NEGATIVE REINFORCEMENT*

Directions: The following five statements are examples of negative reinforcement. Record the antecedent, the behavior, and the consequence provided in the statement.

EXAMPLE: You pay your taxes and you are not sent to jail.
    ANTECEDENT: threat of going to jail
    BEHAVIOR: you pay your taxes
    CONSEQUENCE: avoid going to jail

1. The recreation staff member begins telling Douglas to put his crafts materials away. Douglas puts away the materials and the staff member stops nagging him.

    ANTECEDENT: _____.

    BEHAVIOR: _____.

    CONSEQUENCE: _____.

2. The participants in a music appreciation activity are disruptive and loud. The recreation leader turns the music off and the room becomes silent.

    ANTECEDENT: _____.

    BEHAVIOR: _____.

    CONSEQUENCE: _____.

3. Before going out to the park Carol looks out the window, sees it is raining, and puts on her rain coat.

    ANTECEDENT: _____.

    BEHAVIOR: _____.

    CONSEQUENCE: _____.

4. Ralph joins an activity in the game room and the recreation leader stops coaxing him.

ANTECEDENT: _____.

BEHAVIOR: _____.

CONSEQUENCE: _____.

5. When in a store Gail begins to cry. The staff member buys her a candy bar and she stops crying.

ANTECEDENT: _____.

BEHAVIOR: _____.

CONSEQUENCE: _____.

Directions: Please circle the letter corresponding to the best answer.

6. What are two frequent responses of an individual to an ongoing aversive condition?
   a. avoidance, satiation
   b. depression, escape
   c. escape, avoidance
   d. rejection, aggression
   e. satiation, rejection

7. What is an example of negative reinforcement?
   a. Ross kisses Sue—Sue cries—Ross kisses Sue again.
   b. Steve and Donna sit beside each other—Steve hits Donna— Donna cries.
   c. Sue cries—Ross yells at Sue—Sue continues to cry.
   d. Sue cries—Ross leaves the room—Ross no longer hears Sue cry.
   e. Stephen hits Donna—Donna cries—Ross reprimands Stephen.

8. The result of negative reinforcement is the:
   a. removal of a contingent consequence.
   b. removal of an aversive consequence.
   c. strengthening of a behavior.
   d. weakening of a behavior.
   e. weakening of a conditioned reinforcer.

9. An aversive antecedent is any environmental agent that:
   a. is desired by the person whose behavior is to be reinforced.
   b. is not desired by the person whose behavior is to be reinforced.
   c. is neutral; it has no influence on the target behavior.
   d. will weaken the duration of the target behavior.
   e. will weaken the rate at which the target behavior occurs.

10. Negative reinforcement and positive reinforcement are similar in that both:
    a. depend on the presence of aversive antecedents.
    b. depend on the presentation of a desired consequence.
    c. require conditioned consequences.
    d. will eliminate inappropriate behavior.
    e. will strengthen a behavior.

11. In negative reinforcement, when an individual engages in the appropriate behavior, the aversive condition is:
    a. delivered.
    b. graphed.
    c. measured.
    d. removed.
    e. strengthened.

12. Negative reinforcement and positive reinforcement are not alike in that positive reinforcement involves the delivery of a desired consequence and negative reinforcement involves the:
    a. delivery of an aversive antecedent.
    b. deliver of an aversive consequence.
    c. removal of an aversive condition.
    d. removal of an aversive consequence.
    e. removal of a desired consequence.

13. Escape and avoidance are alike in that both:
    a. depend on the delivery of a desired consequence.
    b. prevent appropriate behavior from occurring.
    c. prevent inappropriate behavior from occurring.
    d. strengthen behavior.
    e. weaken behavior.

14. Escape and avoidance are *not* alike in that escape involves the removal of an aversive condition that is already present and avoidance involves the:
    a. delivery of an aversive condition.
    b. delivery of a desired consequence.
    c. removal of a desired consequence.
    d. removal of an opportunity to engage in inappropriate behavior.
    e. removal of the possibility of an abrasive condition.

15. As a general rule, negative reinforcement:
    a. has a high rate of success in eliminating inappropriate behavior.
    b. has a high rate of success in preventing escape and avoidance.
    c. should be applied as a last resort.
    d. should be applied before positive reinforcement is attempted.
    e. should be applied only as a punitive measure.

Now that you have completed the evaluation, please check your answers with the ones in the back of the book. If needed, review the material on negative reinforcement and try the evaluation again. When you are satisfied with your acquisition of the information and understand your errors, turn the page and begin work on the next chapter.

CHAPTER EIGHT

DECELERATING BEHAVIORS: EXTINCTION

Behavior modification programs not only aim to strengthen certain behaviors by reinforcement, they often seek ways to decrease or eliminate other behaviors that are deemed inappropriate. Inappropriate behaviors take a variety of forms and have a variety of impacts. They may include behaviors that are dangerous or injurious to the individual or others, are extremely disruptive for other people who share the same environment as the individual, are roadblocks to programmed efforts aimed at teaching desired behaviors, or are harmful in other ways. It is important to remember that all behaviors are reinforced in some manner. Inappropriate behaviors may be reinforced by peers, relatives, visitors to programs, well-intentioned but ill-informed staff members, the individuals themselves, or by other agents in the environment. Whatever the source of reinforcement, inappropriate behaviors that prevent an individual from learning how to participate in recreation activities should be decreased.

One of the preferred methods of decreasing an inappropriate behavior is termed EXTINCTION. *Extinction* occurs when the reinforcers which originally maintained a behavior are no longer available to an individual. The essence of the extinction procedure lies in insuring that the reinforcers are WITHHELD that have previously been present following inappropriate behaviors. When a behavior is no longer followed by reinforcement, it gradually diminishes. The application of extinction procedures results in a DECREASE or elimination of the identified inappropriate behavior.

Characteristics of extinction:

1. WITHHOLD previous reinforcers.
2. Results in a DECREASE of behavior.

When an inappropriate behavior has been selected for extinction, it is imperative that ALTERNATIVE positive reinforcers for the inappropriate behaviors are not available for the participant. *Alternative positive reinforcers* are reinforcers other than those that are being withheld. If alternative positive reinforcers are not identified and controlled—if they are in fact present—then extinction is not taking place but rather positive reinforcement of the inappropriate behavior is occurring. Such a circumstance is self-defeating. For example, an adolescent residing in a correctional institution for juvenile offenders may engage in excessively loud burping and belching during the creative arts session. This behavior consistently prompts the instructor to speak to the individual and scold her for her behavior. After this behavior has persisted for several weeks, the instructor is certain that the individual engages in this behavior to force the instructor into focusing his attention on her. The instructor believes that giving his attention to the individual following this inappropriate behavior is reinforcing that behavior; therefore, the instructor decides to extinguish the burping and belching by ignoring those behaviors. However, after several sessions of ignoring the inappropriate behavior, the burping and belching continues unabated because it is also being reinforced by attention and adulation from the individual's peers in the creative arts class. In this case, ALTERNATIVE positive reinforcers are supporting the inappropriate behavior and should be eliminated before there is any possibility of success in extinguishing the inappropriate behavior.

There may be instances when the extinction procedure can be employed by itself, but it is likely that it will be more efficient when it is combined with the POSITIVE REINFORCEMENT of a desired behavior that can be used to replace the identified inappropriate behavior. The positive reinforcement procedure has to be carefully administered. Positive reinforcement cannot be applied immediately after the cessation of the inappropriate behavior; otherwise, it would be reinforcing the very behavior that is to be extinguished. The reinforcement would have to be applied after the individual engaged in the desired behavior. For example, a child in a pre-school play program may cry continuously whenever she is not the object of attention from the play leader. This results in the play leader devoting most of her time and attention to the one child, while neglecting the others. If the play leader would not provide a response to the crying, the crying would eventually wane or cease altogether. Then, after the child had ceased crying for a short period of time and begun playing with a toy, the play leader could positively reinforce the behavior of toy play. It is likely that the combination of ignoring the crying (extinction) and rewarding toy play (positive reinforcement) will result in future instances of less crying and more toy play.

There are other considerations that support the combining of positive reinforcement with extinction. Extinction by itself may result in the weakening or elimination of the inappropriate behavior, but it does nothing to insure that a desired behavior will replace the inappropriate behavior. Positive reinforcement can be used to effect a desired replacement. In addition, if extinction is employed as the sole behavior modification procedure, the odds are high that the inappropriate behavior will return once the extinction procedure is ended. Again, this is likely because there was no positive reinforcement for a desired replacement behavior. Also, when extinction is applied, there is a high possibility of the emergence of other characteristics, such as anger, aggression, frustration, sense of failure or other undesirable emotions. Positive reinforcement can be a mitigating force by lessening the likelihood that these emotions will appear.

It is also important to understand that extinction of a behavior will occur more rapidly if the behavior was reinforced CONTINUOUSLY in the past and extinction will take longer if the behavior was reinforced intermittently in the past. The unfortunate aspect of this principle is that most behaviors are reinforced intermittently and therefore will take longer to extinguish. The basis for this lies in the fact that an individual who has received intermittent reinforcement for an inappropriate behavior is accustomed to experiencing occasions where there was no reinforcement for the behavior. Withholding a reinforcer is not sufficient cause for the individual to immediately consider a modification of behavior because in the past the reinforcer eventually was available and might yet be in the future. Thus, longer periods of time and numerous instances of the behavior without reinforcement are required before the extinction procedure can begin to show results.

Guidelines for the application of extinction:

1. Withhold ALTERNATIVE positive reinforcers.
2. Combine with POSITIVE REINFORCEMENT of desired behaviors.
3. CONTINUOUSLY apply the extinction procedure for numerous instances of the behavior.

There are two characteristics associated with extinction that should be understood before an extinction procedure is implemented. After an extinction procedure is initiated, it is quite common for the inappropriate behavior to increase in some manner. This occurrence is termed an EXTINCTION BURST. An *extinction burst* means the inappropriate behavior will be engaged in more often, more vigorously, or for longer periods of time by the individual in an effort to receive the reinforcer.

75

For example, a camp counselor may encounter a young camper who engages in tantrums. The counselor may decide to attempt to extinguish the tantrums by ignoring them. It is quite likely that the tantrums will increase in duration and intensity. It is important for the counselor to understand that extinction burst may occur and to be prepared to cope with it. If the tantrum increases in severity and the counselor, not being prepared for the outburst, then attends to it, the only result is positive reinforcement of more inappropriate behavior. The setting in which the extinction burst occurs and its effect on others must also receive consideration from the counselor. However, extinction burst will eventually fade and the behavior will gradually diminish.

Another consideration associated with extinction burst is related to the nature of the inappropriate behavior. If the behavior is self-destructive or injurious to the subject, then extinction burst becomes an even greater concern. The likelihood of extinction burst and its impact may result in choosing a behavior modification procedure other than extinction.

After an extinction program has progressed, the behavior may temporarily reappear, even though it has not been reinforced. The temporary recurrence of a non-reinforced behavior during an extinction program is referred to as *spontaneous recovery*. When a behavior recovers during extinction, its strength ordinarily will be less than it was prior to the implementation of the procedure. The major concern during a spontaneous recovery is that the behavior not be reinforced in any way. This would only delay the extinction process and make it more difficult.

Try the following as an exercise to obtain an accurate picture of the phenomena of extinction burst and spontaneous recovery. Assume that Brenda, a university student majoring in recreation, has obtained part-time employment in a neighborhood recreation center. One of the responsibilities assigned to Brenda by the recreation center director is to teach a creative crafts class to elementary school-aged children. The class will be Brenda's first experience in teaching this age group; therefore, the center director decides to unobtrusively observe the class and provide Brenda any assistance and support that is necessary.

On the first day of class the center director notices that when Brenda is giving instructions and guidance, she is frequently interrupted by Paul, a fourth grade student. Brenda deals with each interruption by attending to Paul's questions and comments. The center director decides to observe the class during its next ten sessions and record the number of times Brenda is interrupted by Paul. At the end of the ten sessions the center director's notes provided the following information:

Session	Number of Interruptions
1	8
2	7
3	6
4	7
5	8
6	6
7	8
8	7
9	7
10	8

During a conference between the center director and Brenda, the issue of Paul's behavior was discussed. They determined that action would need to be taken to eliminate or reduce the number of interruptions. It was decided to attempt to extinguish Paul's interruptions, beginning with the 11th class session, by ignoring him (withholding attention) whenever he interrupted and to provide positive reinforcement by giving him some individual attention after he had been on task with his project for an appropriate time. The center director continued to observe Paul's behavior throughout the extinction process. At the conclusion of the creative crafts class, the center director's notes provided this additional information:

Session	Number of Interruptions
11	12
12	11
13	11
14	12
15	10
16	8
17	6
18	4
19	1
20	4
21	5
22	6
23	2
24	0

Using the graph below, construct a graph that depicts the information provided in this exercise. Label the abscissa and ordinate axes and identify the baseline and intervention periods. Record on the graph where the extinction burst and the spontaneous recovery occurred.

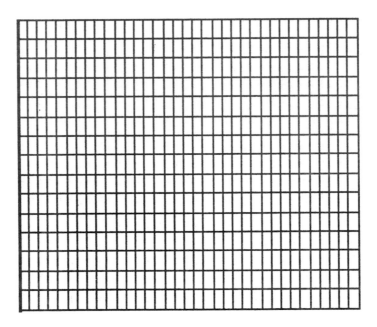

If the completed graph looks like the one on the following page, you did the exercise correctly.

EXTINCTION EXAMPLE

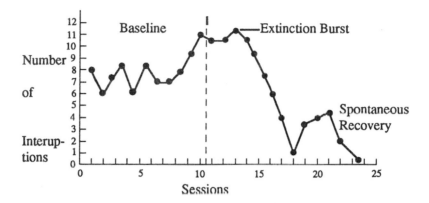

Extinction Burst: An increase in the behavior after initiation of extinction program.

Spontaneous Recovery: A temporary recurrence of a non-reinforced behavior

There are some precautions to heed before selecting extinction as a behavior modification procedure. Because extinction is a gradual process, it may not be the appropriate procedure to employ if quicker results are desired. Also, there are some behaviors that are not prone to extinction. Behaviors that are self-reinforcing are particularly difficult to extinguish.

As an example, a boy in a leisure education class may spend the majority of the class period gazing out the window. This inattentive behavior is effectively obstructing the potential benefits to be gained from the class and the leisure educator may desire to eliminate the behavior by extinguishing it. However, gazing out the window is a self-reinforcing behavior. The pleasure or satisfaction gained from looking out the window reinforces the behavior. In other words, gazing out the window is its own reward. Because it is self-reinforcing, it is not generally susceptible to extinction. The leisure educator would be well-advised to apply an alternative procedure other than extinction to weaken or eliminate the behavior of looking out the window, such as reinforcing behaviors that are incompatible with looking out the window.

In summary, extinction is an appropriate procedure if (a) the reinforcers of the behavior can be identified, (b) the reinforcers can be controlled, and (c) the extinction burst can be tolerated by the individual, the individual's peers, and the person applying the extinction procedure.

To determine the degree to which you have retained the information presented on extinction, go to the next page and complete the evaluation.

TEST YOUR KNOWLEDGE OF *EXTINCTION*

Directions: Please circle the letter that corresponds to the best answer.

1. What is the term used to describe the procedure that leads to an increase of a behavior following the initiation of a successful extinction program?
   a. extinction burst
   b. gradual decrease
   c. positive reinforcement
   d. punishment
   e. spontaneous recovery

2. If an extinction program is effective, what will happen to the target behavior?
   a. be positively reinforced
   b. decrease
   c. increase
   d. remain the same
   e. spontaneously recover

3. What is the term used to describe the temporary recurrence of the inappropriate behavior during extinction?
   a. extinction burst
   b. gradual decrease
   c. positive reinforcer
   d. punisher
   e. spontaneous recovery

4. For which behavior would extinction probably be effective?
   a. banging head against the wall
   b. fighting with other participants
   c. inappropriate verbalizations
   d. knocking equipment over
   e. rocking back and forth

5. During social gatherings Alice often approaches people and talks very close to their faces. An extinction program was established for this inappropriate behavior. If this program is effective, what will you most likely observe immediately following initiation of the program?
   a. a burst of appropriate behaviors will occur
   b. her talking too close will spontaneously recover
   c. she is being reinforced for talking too close
   d. she will avoid talking with others
   e. the frequency of her talking too close increases

6. Extinction is a procedure that may be best described as:
   a. applying negative reinforcement to eliminate inappropriate behavior.
   b. applying positive reinforcement to strengthen a desired behavior.
   c. withholding negative reinforcement to enhance the sources of positive reinforcement for a client.
   d. withholding positive reinforcement to decrease or eliminate inappropriate behaviors.
   e. withholding positive reinforcement to eliminate previously unreinforced behaviors.

7. Within the context of an extinction procedure, alternative positive reinforcers:
   a. do not require identification because they are universally recognized.
   b. are available as "back-up" reinforcers if the first positive reinforcers fail.
   c. are positive reinforcers other than those being deliberately withheld.
   d. are applied as a group to speed the process of eliminating an inappropriate behavior.
   e. are an acceptable substitute for negative reinforcement.

8. Within the context of an extinction procedure, possible alternative positive reinforcers:
   a. may be ignored because they are of no consequence.
   b. must be identified and controlled to insure any chance for success.
   c. are used to elicit desired behaviors.
   d. may be applied to effect a rapid decrease of the target behavior.
   e. are always in the category of primary reinforcers.

9. Extinction occurs when:
   a. reinforcers that had previously maintained a behavior are no longer available and it decreases or ceases altogether.
   b. negative reinforcement is applied to lessen an inappropriate behavior.
   c. negative reinforcement is applied to substitute a desired behavior for an inappropriate behavior.
   d. a behavior decreases because it is subject to rigorous disciplinary measures.
   e. a positive reinforcer loses its ability to maintain a desired behavior.

10. When alternative positive reinforcers are not controlled during an extinction procedure, there is a strong likelihood that:
   a. the inappropriate behavior will decrease.
   b. extinction is not taking place and the target behavior is actually being strengthened by reinforcement.
   c. negative reinforcement will be required to support the extinction procedure.
   d. the extinction procedure will occur more rapidly than may be expected.
   e. extinction burst will not occur.

11. When an extinction procedure is combined with positive reinforcement of a desired behavior, there is a strong likelihood that:
    a. extinction of the inappropriate behavior will proceed more efficiently.
    b. extinction will be delayed because of confusion on the part of the client.
    c. extinction will not occur.
    d. spontaneous recovery will be prevented altogether.
    e. extinction burst will be prevented altogether.

12. When an extinction procedure is combined with positive reinforcement of a desired behavior, there is a strong likelihood that the:
    a. identified inappropriate behavior will be replaced by the desired behavior.
    b. desired behavior will be replaced by the inappropriate behavior.
    c. inappropriate behavior will gradually increase in strength
    d. desired behavior will gradually decrease in strength
    e. inappropriate behavior will require negative reinforcement.

13. When extinction is the sole behavior modification procedure being applied, there is a strong likelihood that:
    a. extinction burst will not occur.
    b. negative reinforcement will soon be required to effect any measurable change in behavior.
    c. the inappropriate behavior may weaken but there is little assurance that it will be replaced by a more desired behavior.
    d. the time required for a successful extinction will be much shorter than otherwise.
    e. spontaneous recovery will not occur.

14. When extinction is the sole behavior modification being applied, there is a strong likelihood that:
    a. a desired replacement behavior will arise spontaneously.
    b. the client will not engage in escape and avoidance activities.
    c. the client will voluntarily seek negative reinforcement.
    d. the inappropriate behavior will return after the extinction process ceases.
    e. the inappropriate behavior will be eradicated quickly.

15. During an extinction process there is a high possibility of the:
    a. person experiencing satiation from negative reinforcement.
    b. emergence in the person of such undesirable characteristics as aggression, anger and frustration.
    c. rapid disappearance of unwanted side-effects such as aggression, anger and frustration.
    d. spontaneous substitution of an inappropriate behavior for a desired behavior.
    e. spontaneous substitution of one desired behavior for another desired behavior.

16. Extinction will occur more rapidly if the target behavior:
    a. is also subjected to positive reinforcement.
    b. is of a physical nature, rather than a social nature.
    c. is supported by negative reinforcement.
    d. was previously reinforced continuously.
    e. was previously reinforced intermittently.

When you have completed the evaluation, please check your answers with those listed in the back of the book. When you are satisfied with your work, please turn the page and begin the next chapter.

CHAPTER NINE

DECELERATING BEHAVIORS: PUNISHMENT

Punishment—like extinction—is a behavior modification procedure that is used to weaken or eliminate an inappropriate behavior. *Punishment* is the presentation of an aversive event or consequence immediately following an instance of inappropriate behavior that leads to a decrease in the occurrence of that behavior. As is the case in other behavior modification procedures, punishment should be used for a specific action or behavior rather than for a general group of behaviors. It is an extreme form of behavior modification that should be used rarely and only after all other courses of action have been tried and found ineffective. The punishment procedure has several limitations and disadvantages but there are occasions where its utilization is justified.

It is essential that individuals employing behavior modification techniques possess a clear understanding of punishment and are able to distinguish the differences between punishment and extinction, as well as the differences between punishment and negative reinforcement. Both punishment and extinction are used to weaken or eliminate a behavior but punishment involves the presentation (or addition) of an aversive event following an instance of a behavior and extinction involves the non-presentation (or removal) of reinforcers that had previously been available to maintain a behavior. The intent of punishment and extinction are similar; the intent of punishment and negative reinforcement are opposite. Punishment is used to decrease an inappropriate behavior; negative reinforcement is used to increase a desired behavior. Punishment involves the addition of an aversive event. Negative reinforcement involves the removal or postponement of an aversive event, contingent on the occurrences of a behavior.

Punishment should not be applied in isolation. Rather, it should be an integral part of a well-planned program. One of the criticisms commonly levied against punishment is that it teaches the individual to whom it is being applied only what not to do; it does not teach the individual what to do by assisting in the development of desired alternate behavior. Therefore, punishment should always be used

IN CONJUNCTION WITH POSITIVE REINFORCEMENT that will provide the individual with acceptable alternate behavior. Prior to the initiation of a punishment procedure, desired alternate behaviors should be identified and plans formulated for establishing and reinforcing them. As part of this plan, there should also be an attempt to discover what prompts the inappropriate behavior and what reinforcers are maintaining it. On occasion, identification and control of these two factors will result in the emergence of a desired alternative behavior and the application of a punisher becomes unnecessary.

A comprehensive approach that includes both punishment and positive reinforcement must be carefully implemented. Care must be taken to insure that positive reinforcement is used only with the desired alternate behavior. The pitfall that must be avoided is delivering the punisher in such a manner that it can be associated with the positive reinforcer. If this occurs, the positive reinforcer may offset the impact of the punisher and it may also reinforce the inappropriate behavior that is to be eliminated. However, there are substantial advantages to be gained from positive reinforcement in instances where punishment is also part of the approach. Positive reinforcement can also make the punisher more effective, which will lead to a more rapid weakening of the inappropriate behavior. In addition, positive reinforcement also has the potential to mitigate some of the undesirable side effects that are always a possibility whenever punishment is applied.

Important concerns related to punishment:

1. Never use punishment in ISOLATION.
2. Always use punishment in CONJUNCTION WITH POSITIVE REINFORCEMENT of desired behaviors.

Choosing an aversive event to serve as the punisher is an important part of the punishment procedure. There are several guidelines that should be followed in selecting a punisher. Observance of these guidelines will help to insure optimum results from applying the procedure. First, it is essential that the event selected to serve as the punisher is AVERSIVE and effective in decreasing the behavior. It is possible that what is generally regarded by most people to be an aversive event may not, in fact, be aversive for the individual to whom it is applied. An aversive event may be deemed a punisher only if it is successful in effecting a decrease in the target behavior. Second, the aversive event must be POWERFUL enough to serve as a punisher. Presenting the aversive event in a MILD form with the thought that, if necessary, it can be applied in stronger forms in the future is not a good technique. If the aversive event is too mild, it may not be a punisher. Gradually increasing its strength in subsequent applications may result only in the gradual loss of its effectiveness. A better approach to the issue is to carefully determine what the strength of the aversive event should be and then present it at that level for its first, and all subsequent, applications. Determining the strength of a punisher requires sound professional judgment. The punisher needs to be strong enough to be effective but, at the same time, nothing is gained from using a stronger punisher when a mild one will achieve the same results. In addition, when administering the punishment, the recreation professional should make the punisher as BRIEF as possible and require MINIMAL SOCIAL INTERACTION. Frequently, individuals will exhibit inappropriate behaviors in an attempt to gain attention which they view as a positive reinforcer. If this is the case, the more attention the professional administering the intended punisher provides the individual, the more likely the person will view the situation as reinforcing rather than punishing.

Guidelines for choosing punishers:

1. Must be AVERSIVE to the individual.
2. Must be POWERFUL enough to affect behavior.
3. Should be as MILD as possible.
4. Should be BRIEF.
5. Should require MINIMAL SOCIAL INTERACTION.

The presentation—or delivery—of the punisher is also an important part of the punishment procedure and there are guidelines to be followed here as well. First, the punisher should be applied IMMEDIATELY after the individual has engaged in the target behavior. If the punishment is delayed, there is the possibility that the individual will, in the interim, have engaged in an entirely appropriate or desired behavior. If punishment is then delivered, the individual may be confused as to which behavior is being punished. Second, the punisher should CONSISTENTLY be presented following each instance of the target behavior. Intermittent punishment is not effective. A significant implication related to this guideline is that each instance of the behavior needs to be capable of detection. If all instances of the behavior are not detected, punishment will probably not be an effective behavior modifier. Third, the person delivering the punisher must never do so in anger but always CALMLY and with a steady demeanor. If there is even the slightest hint of revenge or retribution in the application of the punisher, the entire procedure should be carefully reviewed. Fourth, the person presenting the punisher should be one who also applies positive reinforcement for desired alternate behavior. The use of the punishment UNIFORMLY across all personnel will reduce the likelihood of the presenters being perceived as a conditioned punisher.

Guidelines for administering punishment:

1. IMMEDIATELY.
2. CONSISTENTLY.
3. CALMLY.
4. UNIFORMLY.

The possibility of the emergence of a CONDITIONED PUNISHER is but one of several weaknesses and disadvantages associated with the punishment procedure. *A conditioned punisher* is any person, object, event, or other environmental factor that is allied with the punisher and becomes, through association, a punisher itself. If the person applying the punisher is perceived as a CONDITIONED PUNISHER, that person's role as a provider of reinforcement for desirable alternative behavior is seriously diminished. This is extremely important to recreation professionals attempting to provide an enjoyable atmosphere conducive for learning leisure skills. If the recreation professional administers punishment, the participants may develop a negative image of that person. This negative image may inhibit participants' ability to enjoy activities when the recreation professional is in attendance.

Another disadvantage of the punishment procedure is that when an individual is punished, that individual often attempts to ESCAPE or AVOID the place where the punishment occurred or the person who applied the punisher. This introduces another element into the punishment procedure, one that is related to efficient use of time. Time spent by a behavior modification staff trying to counteract escape and avoidance techniques used by the subject is time that cannot be spent in trying to develop desired alternate behavior.

If the individual is unable to escape or avoid a punishment, aggression may surface. AGGRESSION is another disadvantage of the procedure. People who are punished may attack persons or objects present at the time, especially the person who is doing the punishing. The aggression may be verbal or physical. Another weakness of the punishment procedure is the likelihood that, with continued use, a punisher may LOSE ITS EFFECTIVENESS and the punished behavior may return to its original rate. This is especially true of punishers that are not very intense.

There is an additional drawback associated with the use of punishment that merits consideration. Punishment often results in a relatively rapid decrease in the target behavior. Because of the quick results obtained by the use of punishment, the possibility exists that it may become a procedure that is TOO READILY APPLIED when another procedure might be more appropriate.

Disadvantages of punishment:

1. CONDITIONED PUNISHER
2. ESCAPE
3. AVOIDANCE
4. AGGRESSION
5. LOSE EFFECTIVENESS
6. TOO READILY APPLIED

Try this as an exercise to review the weaknesses and disadvantages of the punishment procedure. Each of the six following paragraphs describes a situation in which punishment is applied and a disadvantage of the procedure emerges. On the lines following each paragraph, enter the disadvantage that became apparent.

Situation 1. The dining hall in a resident camp is an older building with small, narrow entrances. Because of this, campers often have to stand in line at meal time while waiting their turn to get into the dining hall. Jerry, an older camper, does not like to wait and tries to crowd in at the head of the line. His cabin counselor informs him that because of his crowding in ahead of others, he will be assigned to latrine clean-up for the next week. Jerry doesn't like the idea of having to do extra latrine duty and, while leaving the dining hall, bullies younger campers by shoving them out of his way and pushing them to the ground.

Situation 2. A summer playground program has attracted several neighborhood children, a few of whom are of kindergarten age. One of the favorite activities of the kindergarten children is to play in a sandbox, making forts, castles, and other structures. Cindy, one of the older neighborhood children, gets into the sandbox and knocks down the castle the kindergarten children are making. The playground leader sees this and begins walking in the direction of the sandbox. Cindy sees the leader coming and runs off the playground toward home.

Situation 3. The Saturday morning children's hikes sponsored by the nature center are very popular. Because of the large number of hikers, it is often difficult for the interpretive naturalist to command the silence that is required when the group is listening for bird calls. When the naturalist hears two hikers talking and laughing loudly, she sends them back to the center. This action subdues the remainder of the hikers. Subsequently, when the naturalist spots any disturbance among the hikers, she sends the culprits back to the center building. This immediately quiets the other hikers.

Situation 4. As part of a leisure education class, Jim is learning to play card games. While playing, he is allowed to listen to a pocket radio with its own set of headphones. If Jim becomes frustrated with the game he is playing, he throws his cards on the floor. When that happens, the instructor requires Jim to remove his headphones and turn off the radio. This prompts Jim to pick up the cards and resume playing. However, as the sessions continue, Jim still throws his cards on the floor, even after his radio has been removed from his person.

Situation 5. During a free-play period in the gymnasium of a local recreation center, the supervisor momentarily leaves the gym to answer a phone call. In his absence one of the boys takes a big mouthful of water from the drinking fountain and spits it on a group of his companions. The supervisor returns to the gym just in time to see this. He begins to chastise the boy and tell him he must wipe the water off the floor. While he is scolding the boy, the boy runs out of the gym and leaves the recreation center.

Situation 6. On the first day of tryouts for the swimming team, the coach and her assistant are faced with a large number of candidates, some of whom are unruly. While attempting to explain her rules and procedures to the swimmers, the coach notices that two of the swimmers are trying to throw each other into the pool. She yells at them and tells her assistant to make them stay after practice is over to swim 15 extra laps. The two swimmers are often caught violating the rules and each time the coach has her assistant supervise the extra laps they have to swim after practice. The two swimmers begin to avoid the assistant coach.

If you identified aggression as the disadvantage in situation 1, avoidance in situation 2, too easily applied in situation 3, loses effectiveness in situation 4, escape in situation 5, and conditioned punisher in situation 6, you have a good command of the weaknesses and disadvantages of the punishment procedure.

Because of the aforementioned disadvantages in using punishment, this consequence should only be used when the behavior endangers the person or others, the behavior results in significant property damage, or when alternate treatment methods have been tried and proved unsuccessful.

To determine the degree to which you have retained the information presented on punishment, go to the next page and complete the evaluation.

TEST YOUR KNOWLEDGE OF *PUNISHMENT*

Directions: Please circle the letter which corresponds to the best answer.

1. What should occur to the behavior if a punishment procedure is effective?
   a. decreases
   b. increases
   c. is negatively reinforced
   d. is positively reinforced
   e. remains the same

2. What will often occur if people are unable to escape or avoid a punisher?
   a. their behaviors will extinguish
   b. their behaviors will be punished
   c. their behaviors will be reinforced
   d. they will become aggressive
   e. they will feel ashamed

3. What characteristics should an effective punisher possess?
   a. brief in duration
   b. consistent, long lasting
   c. escapable, avoidable
   d. immediate, physically painful
   e. negatively reinforcing, specific

4. What is the term used to describe the consequence that occur when an aversive event is added to a behavior and the behavior decreases?
   a. extinction
   b. negative reinforcement
   c. positive reinforcement
   d. punishment
   e. shaping

5. Punishment is a behavior modification technique used to:
   a. chastise an individual for wrong-doing.
   b. strengthen a desired behavior.
   c. strengthen an inappropriate behavior.
   d. weaken a desired behavior.
   e. weaken or eliminate an inappropriate behavior.

6. The punishment procedure involves the presentation of:
   a. a negative reinforcer to weaken an inappropriate behavior.
   b. a positive reinforcer to weaken an inappropriate behavior.
   c. an aversive event to strengthen a desired behavior.
   d. an aversive event to weaken an inappropriate behavior.
   e. physical measures to ensure compliance with rules and regulations by participants.

7. Punishment and extinction are alike in that they both:
   a. are used to strengthen a desired behavior.
   b. are used to weaken or eliminate an inappropriate behavior.
   c. have an element of revenge or retribution.
   d. involve negative reinforcement.
   e. rely on physical measures to ensure compliance with rules and regulations.

8. Punishment differs from extinction in that punishment:
   a. always involves physical measures and extinction never uses physical measures.
   b. involves the addition of an aversive event following the target behavior and extinction involves the removal of reinforcers that had previously maintained a behavior.
   c. is used to strengthen a behavior and extinction is used to weaken a behavior.
   d. is used to weaken a behavior and extinction is used to strengthen a behavior.
   e. uses negative reinforcement and extinction requires the use of positive reinforcement.

9. Punishment differs from negative reinforcement in that punishment:
   a. always uses physical measures and negative reinforcement never employs such means.
   b. can be applied to any violation of rules and regulations and negative reinforcement must focus on a specific behavior.
   c. implies revenge and negative reinforcement does not.
   d. is used to strengthen a desired behavior and negative reinforcement is used to weaken a desired behavior.
   e. is used to weaken an inappropriate behavior and negative reinforcement is used to strengthen a desired behavior.

10. A common criticism of the punishment procedure is:
    a. it is necessary to use corporal punishment.
    b. it isn't used often enough.
    c. it never works as planned.
    d. it only teaches what not to do and does not assist in teaching what to do.
    e. the physical measures are often too strong.

11. Punishment should always be used in association with other behavior modification procedures. This increases the possibility that:
    a. acceptable alternate behavior will be established in place of the inappropriate behavior.
    b. negative reinforcement will be used to weaken the target behavior
    c. punishment can be applied as often as the staff desires.
    d. the physical measures used in punishment will not get out of hand.
    e. the punishment procedure will only have to be used once.

12. When punishment and positive reinforcement are used in conjunction with each other, it is likely that:
    a. neither procedure will work because they will cancel each other's effectiveness.
    b. the positive reinforcer will involve the inflicting of a slight degree of physical discomfort on the participant.
    c. the punisher will become less effective and delay the weakening of the inappropriate behavior.
    d. the punisher will become more effective and hasten the weakening of the inappropriate behavior.
    e. the punisher will involve the inflicting of a slight degree of physical discomfort on the participant.

13. In selecting an aversive event as a punisher, it is important to ensure that:
    a. each staff member has his/her own aversive event to present to the participant.
    b. it effectively strengthens the alternate behavior.
    c. it effectively weakens the inappropriate behavior.
    d. it is mild enough to prevent any distress or discomfort in the participant.
    e. it is the same aversive event that is applied in all punishment procedures for all program participants.

14. In presenting an aversive event to a participant, an important guideline to follow is the:
    a. punisher should alternate between strong and mild forms.
    b. punisher should start out in its mildest form and then gradually increase in strength.
    c. punisher should start out in its strongest form and then gradually decrease in strength.
    d. strength of the punisher should be changed at random.
    e. strength of the punisher should be the same for the initial and all subsequent applications.

15. In presenting an aversive event to a participant, another important guideline to follow is the:
    a. participant should never know how the punishment is being applied.
    b. punisher should always involve some slight physical discomfort for the participant.
    c. punisher should be applied immediately after the participant has engaged in the inappropriate behavior.
    d. punisher should be delayed in order to allow the situation to cool down.
    e. staff members should make an on-the-spot judgment as to whether or not it should be applied.

16. A conditioned punisher is:
    a. a second punisher that is applied if the first one proves to be ineffective.
    b. always a physical measure designed to improve the general state of affairs.
    c. one that can be applied only under certain conditions.
    d. one that has lost its effectiveness.
    e. some thing that is allied with the punisher and, through association, becomes a punisher itself.

17. A disadvantage of the punishment procedure is that:
    a. conditioned punishers never emerge spontaneously.
    b. corporal punishment is prohibited in some instances and this reduces the effectiveness of the procedure.
    c. it doesn't work well when used in conjunction with positive reinforcement.
    d. it works too rapidly to allow the participant time to assimilate what is happening.
    e. the participant often tries to escape or avoid the punishment.

18. Another disadvantage of the punishment procedure is the likelihood of:
    a. a specific behavior being targeted for weakening or elimination, rather than a general group of inappropriate behaviors.
    b. an increase in inappropriate behavior by the participant as a means of gaining attention.
    c. permanent harm to the participant because of extreme physical measures.
    d. the emergence of aggression in the participant.
    e. the emergence of docile and submissive behavior in the participant.

When you have completed the evaluation, check your answers with the ones listed in the back of the book. When you are satisfied with your retention of the material related to punishment, please turn the page to begin work on the next chapter.

CHAPTER TEN

DECELERATING BEHAVIORS: WITHDRAWAL OF REINFORCEMENT

There are procedures other than extinction and punishment that can be used to decelerate inappropriate behaviors. Two additional procedures are RESPONSE COST and TIME-OUT FROM POSITIVE REINFORCEMENT. Depending on the circumstances, any of these procedures can be effective and appropriate to use. Therapeutic recreation specialists who are familiar with the characteristics of each of these procedures can generally deal with most instances of undesired behavior. This, in turn, allows participants to benefit as much as possible from leisure services.

Response cost is a behavior modification procedure that may be applied to effect a reduction in undesirable or inappropriate behavior. *Response cost* involves the REMOVAL of a specified quantity of reinforcement from an individual, CONTINGENT on the performance of a target behavior. It is an aversive procedure in that it involves taking away positive reinforcers an individual has accumulated. Because it is an aversive procedure, it should be employed only after the utilization of alternative procedures has proven to be ineffective. Possible legal and moral issues related to the application of response cost should receive careful consideration.

Because response cost involves the removal of reinforcement an individual has accumulated, it is most often applied in circumstances where the reinforcers are in the form of tokens. Items that can be exchanged for something the individual desires are typically used because reinforcers in the form of something edible or capable of being used immediately might be consumed or otherwise expended by the individual before response cost can be applied.

Response cost is similar to punishment in that both procedures are aversive in nature and are applied as techniques to bring about a reduction in inappropriate behavior. However, response cost differs significantly from punishment in a major way. *Punishment* involves the presentation of an aversive event, contingent upon the exhibition of

101

inappropriate behavior by an individual. Response cost involves the REMOVAL of a specified QUANTITY of reinforcement that has already been given to an individual, CONTINGENT upon the person's inappropriate behavior. For example, if a boy in a crafts class disrupts the other participants in the class by throwing objects at them and is then required by the instructor to sweep the craftroom floor, there is an application of the punishment procedure. On the other hand, if that boy had been accumulating points in a system where 100 points could be exchanged for a box of raisins and the instructor subtracted 25 points from his total for throwing objects, that is an application of the response cost procedure. Both procedures are aversive, but punishment involves presentation of an aversive event and response cost involves removal of a quantity of reinforcers.

When considering the use of response cost it is important to remember that the procedure involves:

1. the REMOVAL of
2. a specified QUANTITY of reinforcement,
3. CONTINGENT on the performance of a target behavior.

There are several factors that should be considered when contemplating the use of response cost. First, because the central feature of response cost is the removal of a specified quantity of the reinforcers an individual has, it follows that the individual must be given an opportunity to ACCUMULATE a reserve of reinforcers. For example, if the reinforcers are tokens, the individual must be allowed a chance to acquire a supply of tokens before a response cost procedure is initiated. The accumulation of tokens should not be too difficult to achieve, since tokens are generally used to reinforce weak behaviors and individuals are generally afforded many chances to acquire them. If an individual has had an opportunity to cash in tokens for the back-up reinforcers, response cost may have its strongest effect because the individual, after having seen what can be gained by the tokens, should try harder to avoid losing them.

Second, the SIZE of the penalty (the quantity of reinforcers to be removed) must be determined beforehand and applied consistently. The size of the penalty should be determined on a case-by-case basis. Some individuals may require a large penalty; other individuals may respond to a small penalty. The history of the individual will have to be considered, the inappropriate behavior closely observed, and penalties of various magnitude tried until an appropriate one is determined. It should be noted that there is nothing to be gained by the imposition of a large penalty if a small penalty is equally effective in reducing the inappropriate behavior.

When attempting to determine the appropriate quantity for the penalty, it is ineffective to increase the size by small amounts. Gradual increases allow individuals the opportunity to make adaptations to the penalty. It is better to return to a zero penalty for a reassessment of the procedure or quickly go to a much stronger penalty and monitor its effects.

Third, if response cost is to be applied effectively, the individual participating in the program must be fully INFORMED of the procedure. This person must be informed of the inappropriate behavior that has been targeted for deceleration and the subsequent penalty for engaging in the behavior. In addition to being an equitable way to conduct a response cost system, it allows individuals to be more directly involved in controlling their behaviors.

Fourth, response cost should not be used as an isolated procedure. It will be much more effective if it is used IN CONJUNCTION WITH REINFORCEMENT of desired alternate behaviors. It is possible that the combination of response cost and reinforcement of desired alternate behaviors may soon eliminate the need for the response cost procedure.

Guidelines for the application of response cost:

1. Allow individuals the opportunity to ACCUMULATE a reinforcer reserve.
2. The SIZE of the penalty must be determined on a case-by-case basis.
3. Individuals must be INFORMED of the procedure and the penalties.
4. Response cost should be used IN CONJUNCTION WITH REINFORCEMENT.

There are several advantages associated with the use of response cost. Response cost is a procedure that generally shows immediate results. There have been many instances where response cost has been effective in RAPIDLY reducing inappropriate behaviors. This attribute contributes to the popularity of response cost as a procedure in applied settings. Response cost also has potential for reducing inappropriate behaviors for considerable periods of time. In many cases it has been reported that the application of response cost has resulted in LONG-LASTING reduction of inappropriate behavior. In addition, response cost is a procedure that can be applied IMMEDIATELY. When an individual engages in inappropriate behavior, the removal of a

103

portion of the reinforcers can occur instantaneously. Finally, response cost is a CONVENIENT procedure to use. It can be applied quietly and with a minimum of physical effort and disruption.

The advantages of response cost are:

1. Works RAPIDLY.
2. Has potential for LONG-LASTING effects.
3. Can be applied IMMEDIATELY.
4. Is CONVENIENT to apply.

There are some disadvantages associated with the use of response cost. Because it is so convenient to apply, the potential exists for response cost to be APPLIED TOO READILY. It is possible that it may be applied without exploring the use of alternate procedures or not in conjunction with other, more positive procedures.

There is also a danger that the penalty (the amount of reinforcers that is to be removed) may be TOO LARGE. It is true that a substantial penalty may be required to reduce the target behavior, but it is also true that it may reduce some desirable behaviors as well. For example, an instructor may levy a sizable penalty for inappropriate responses to questions in a leisure education session. This may prevent an individual from uttering inappropriate responses but it may also inhibit the individual from saying anything at all. This would be counterproductive and the leisure education instructor would be well-advised to reassess the procedure and the penalty.

The use of response cost may generate OTHER INAPPROPRIATE BEHAVIORS. An individual may exhibit aggressive behavior toward the person who is conducting the response cost procedure. In addition, the individual may attempt to escape or avoid the entire recreation program. These behaviors would create considerable problems when attempting to develop recreation skills.

As described earlier, an individual must have accumulated a reserve of reinforcers. If an individual eventually has NO MORE REINFORCERS to be taken away, response cost cannot be applied.

Remember, the disadvantages of response cost are:

1. May be APPLIED TOO READILY.
2. May use penalties that are TOO LARGE.
3. May GENERATE OTHER INAPPROPRIATE BEHAVIOR.
4. Individual may have NO MORE REINFORCERS from which a quantity can be removed.

Another procedure that facilitates the deceleration of an undesired behavior is termed TIME-OUT FROM POSITIVE REINFORCEMENT. As with response cost, time-out from positive reinforcement involves the REMOVAL of a reinforcer that results in a decreased rate of behavior. However, *time-out from positive reinforcement* refers specifically to a FIXED PERIOD OF TIME that an individual is placed in an environment that is less reinforcing than the previous environment. The placement of the individual in the less reinforcing environment must occur CONTINGENT on the performance of a target behavior (a target behavior that requires deceleration). An individual's environment can be made less reinforcing by either making the existing environment less reinforcing (e.g., removal of toys for a brief duration, termination of music for a specified time period, termination of interaction between a leader and participant for a few minutes) or moving the person to a less reinforcing environment (e.g., the participant can be required to stand a few feet from the other participants, sit facing a corner of the room, or remain in an empty room for a brief time period). It is important to remember that each of the aforementioned applications of time-out from positive reinforcement must occur in response to a target behavior that should be decreased.

When considering the use of time-out from positive reinforcement it is important to remember that the procedure involves:

1. The REMOVAL of a reinforcer,
2. For a FIXED PERIOD OF TIME,
3. CONTINGENT on the performance of a target behavior.

There are problems associated with time-out from positive reinforcement related to the inability of people to participate in recreation activities during this time. As a result, extinction and response cost are more preferred techniques when attempting to decelerate behaviors. If time-out from positive reinforcement is chosen, the following three important factors affecting the implementation should be considered: (a) DURATION, (b) LOCATION, and (c) ENVIRONMENTAL STIMULATION.

Because participation in the program is the goal of all recreation professionals, it is important to provide an individual with the opportunity to return to the program AS SOON AS POSSIBLE. Once the person returns to the original environment it is important for the therapeutic recreation specialist to reinforce the participant's appropriate behaviors. Typically, the most successful time-out from positive reinforcement procedures do not last very long (5 to 10 minutes at the most).

When moving a person to a less reinforcing environment, the specialist has some options. A person can be moved away from the activity, but observation of the individuals participating in the activity is allowed to continue (e.g., standing a few feet away from participants playing charades). Another alternative is to allow the individual to remain in the room but prevent direct visual observation to occur (e.g., sitting in a chair that faces the corner of the gymnasium while others play volleyball). In addition, a person can be quickly escorted from the room and required to remain in an empty room (e.g., sitting in an empty shelter while the group attempts an outdoor ropes course). Often the placement of the individual in an empty room is the most effective location. However, it is important in this situation that the leader CLOSELY MONITOR the individual during the time-out from positive reinforcement procedure period. If the individual is placed in an empty room the room must not be locked; it should be properly ventilated and lighted, and measure at least 6 feet by 6 feet.

The greater the CONTRAST between the time-out from positive reinforcement environment and the original environment, the more successful the attempts at reducing a behavior will be. Therefore, it is critical to make the environment used for time-out from positive reinforcement as non-stimulating as possible. It is also very important for the specialist to attempt to consistently provide activities that are as interesting as possible. The recreation environment should provide the opportunity for participants to readily obtain positive reinforcement contingent on appropriate behaviors.

When implementing time-out from positive reinforcement it is useful to:

1. Allow the person to return to the activity AS SOON AS POSSIBLE,
2. CLOSELY MONITOR the individual, and
3. Create a time-out environment that is in direct CONTRAST with the recreation environment.

It appears useful at this time to attempt to clarify the difference between time-out from positive reinforcement and extinction. To distinguish between the two procedures, it is helpful to examine what occurs to the environment after the target behavior occurs. In the case of extinction the environment remains the same following the target behavior (e.g., a leader ignores the loud vocalization of a participant and continues to speak to the group). With time-out from positive reinforcement THE ENVIRONMENT CHANGES AFTER THE TARGET BEHAVIOR HAS OCCURRED (e.g., the leader requires the individual to stand outside the crafts room for two minutes).

To distinguish between applications of extinction and time-out from positive reinforcement it is also helpful to examine what happens to reinforcement during these two procedures. In the case of extinction a reinforcer that usually follows a behavior is withheld. With time-out from positive reinforcement A REINFORCER THAT IS ALREADY PRESENT IS TEMPORARILY REMOVED. For instance, suppose a leader has established a rule that if participants arrive on time for a leisure education class they can spend the last ten minutes playing video games. If a participant arrived late to class and could not play video games at the end of class, that would be an application of extinction. However, time-out from positive reinforcement would occur if a participant arrived on time, was playing videos at the end of class, started breaking rules by screaming loudly and then was required to stop playing the videos for the next five minutes.

Time-out from positive reinforcement differs from extinction in the following ways:

1. THE ENVIRONMENT CHANGES AFTER THE TARGET BEHAVIOR HAS OCCURRED, and
2. A REINFORCER THAT IS ALREADY PRESENT IS REMOVED.

Time-out from positive reinforcement and response cost are similar in that both procedures are used to effect a reduction in inappropriate behavior and both involve the REMOVAL of reinforcement CONTINGENT upon the exhibition of inappropriate behavior. However, time out from positive reinforcement involves the withdrawal of reinforcement for a specific AMOUNT OF TIME; response cost involves the withdrawal of a SPECIFIC QUANTITY of reinforcers.

Try this as an exercise. Following are some examples of behavior modification procedures used to decelerate behaviors. On the line following each example, indicate whether the procedure applied was (a) extinction, (b) punishment, (c) response cost, or (d) time-out from positive reinforcement.

1. During a free-swim period, William begins to bully other swimmers by forcing their heads under water. The lifeguard makes William get out of the pool and sit on a bench on the deck for five minutes.

2. The leisure education instructor brings her class to a neighborhood park for a picnic. During the picnic, Norma persists in crowding ahead of all the others to roast her hot dogs. The leisure education instructor tells Norma that crowding in ahead of others is rude and, as a result, she must pick up all the litter that is in their picnic area and deposit it in the trash cans.

3. At Sunnybrook Camp the campers have the opportunity to earn points by keeping their personal living areas neat and clean. The camper can then trade a specified number of points for the right to participate in an activity of choice. Ellen is trying to accumulate 100 points to exchange for an all-day trail ride. However, she fails to make her bunk before going to breakfast. The cabin counselor then deducts 10 points from Ellen's total.

4. During softball practice Margaret tries to hit other players with the ball by throwing it at them when they are not looking. The coach asks Margaret not to do that because she may injure someone. Margaret agrees but tries to do it one more time. The coach tells Margaret that when practice is over she cannot leave with her friends but must stay, gather the equipment, and put it in the van.

5. On the playground James likes to attract the attention of the leader by climbing the ladder to the top of the slide and then start crying, saying he is afraid to go down the slide or climb back down the ladder. The leader then climbs the ladder and brings James back down. The leader soon discovers that James does this two to three times a day. After deciding that James could safely go down the slide or climb down the ladder,

the leader pays no attention when James cries at the top of the slide ladder.

---

6. In the television viewing room Ian is watching television by himself. He turns the volume on the set to its maximum level. A staff member tells Ian the sound is too loud for the crafts class that is meeting in the next room and turns the volume down. Ian turns the volume back up to the maximum level. The staff member then turns the set off and tells Ian that he cannot watch television until 10 minutes have passed.

---

7. John is participating in a bird identification class at the nature center. On nature walks, John is given a small wooden disc with a picture of a bird on it if he is quiet when a bird is calling. If John can accumulate 15 discs, he can trade them for a soft drink at the nature center. However, on the next walk John is talking loudly and otherwise making noise while a bird is calling. The leader takes away three of the discs for each instance of talking and noise-making.

---

8. In exercise classes in the gymnasium Mary has developed the annoying habit of asking the instructor to repeat every set of directions he gives. The instructor complies with each of Mary's requests for the first three exercise sessions but then decides to ignore all of her requests for repeated directions in the future.

If you indicated that examples 1 and 6 are applications of time-out from positive reinforcement, examples 2 and 4 are applications of punishment, examples 3 and 7 are applications of response cost, and examples 5 and 8 are applications of extinction, you provided the correct response for each example.

You have now completed the material on response cost and time-out from positive reinforcement. Please go to the next page and evaluate how well you retained the information.

TEST YOUR KNOWLEDGE OF *RESPONSE COST AND TIME-OUT FROM POSITIVE REINFORCEMENT*

Directions: Please circle the letter that corresponds to the best answer.

1. Response cost involves:
   a. ignoring an individual as a penalty for engaging in inappropriate behavior.
   b. requiring an individual to cease participating in a favorite activity for a specified period of time.
   c. requiring an individual to leave the premises as a result of engaging in inappropriate behavior.
   d. rewarding an individual for engaging in appropriate behavior.
   e. taking away some of the reinforcers an individual has already amassed.

2. Response cost is an aversive procedure because it:
   a. assesses a penalty against an individual.
   b. cannot be used in conjunction with positive reinforcement.
   c. involves a permanent withdrawal of all positive reinforcement.
   d. involves a withdrawal of all negative reinforcement.
   e. requires individuals to cease participation in a favorite activity for a specified period of time.

3. Response cost and punishment are similar in that both procedures:
   a. are used to strengthen weak behaviors.
   b. are used to weaken inappropriate behaviors.
   c. use negative reinforcement.
   d. use positive reinforcement.
   e. withhold primary reinforcers.

4. Response cost and punishment are different in that:
   a. punishment involves the presentation of an aversive event and response cost involves the withholding of a specified amount of reinforcers.
   b. punishment involves the use of extinction and response cost involves the use of negative reinforcement.
   c. response cost involves the presentation of an aversive event and punishment involves the withholding of a specified amount of reinforcers.
   d. response cost involves the use of negative reinforcement and punishment involves the presentation of an aversive event.
   e. response cost involves the use of positive reinforcement and punishment involves the use of negative reinforcement.

5. In order for response cost to be effective, it is essential that:
   a. edible reinforcers be used so the individual will clearly understand the impact of the penalty.
   b. it come as a surprise to the individual, thereby making a stronger impression.
   c. only primary reinforcers are used in the procedure.
   d. the individual to whom it is to be applied has opportunities to build a reinforcer reserve.
   c. the size of the penalty is determined on the spot, thereby making the punishment fit the transgression.

6. After determining that the size of a penalty in response cost should be increased, it is most effective to:
   a. allow the circumstances surrounding the inappropriate behavior to determine the magnitude of the penalty.
   b. gradually increase the penalty by small amounts.
   c. increase the penalty in conjunction with a punishment procedure.
   d. increase the penalty in conjunction with negative reinforcement.
   e. increase the penalty by a substantial amount and do it all in one step.

7. Response cost is most effective when it is used in conjunction with:
   a. deprivation of reinforcement of desired alternate behavior.
   b. extinction of other inappropriate behaviors.
   c. punishment of other inappropriate behaviors.
   d. reinforcement of desired alternate behavior.
   e. satiation.

8. Which of the following is an advantage of using response cost:
   a. individuals to whom it is applied will not engage in escape or avoidance techniques.
   b. it requires no pre-planning.
   c. once the size of a penalty has been determined, it can be applied to all individuals and obtain uniform results.
   d. it is easy to apply.
   e. there are no hazards involved in imposing too large a penalty.

9. Which of the following is a disadvantage of using response cost:
   a. it can generate aggressive behavior in the individual to whom it is applied.
   b. it can only be applied in clinical settings.
   c. it is difficult to apply the procedure.
   d. it requires the use of edible reinforcers.
   e. the procedure takes too long to have any effect.

10. Time-out from positive reinforcement involves:
    a. cessation of a reinforcement program because an individual no longer requires it.
    b. moving an individual into an environment where satiation is likely to occur.
    c. taking away a portion of the reinforcer an individual has already amassed.
    d. the cessation of positive reinforcement and the implementation of negative reinforcement.
    e. the withdrawal of reinforcers for a specified period of time.

11. Time-out from positive reinforcement is used to:
    a. give therapeutic recreation personnel a rest from their duties.
    b. increase the effectiveness of response cost.
    c. reduce an inappropriate behavior.
    d. strengthen an appropriate behavior.
    e. withdraw a specified amount of reinforcers from an individual.

12. Time-out from positive reinforcement should be applied:
    a. contingent upon the exhibition of the target behavior by an individual.
    b. in conjunction with response cost.
    c. when individuals are bored with their environment.
    d. when individuals are physically weary from their activities.
    e. whenever a therapeutic recreation specialist wants to apply it.

13. When considering the application of time-out from positive reinforcement, the duration of the procedure should be:
    a. a relatively brief period of time, five to ten minutes, so the individual can return to participation in the program and receive its benefits.
    b. an extended period of time, at least one hour, so the individual feels the impact.
    c. determined by the mood of the therapeutic recreation specialist.
    d. for a long period of time initially, then gradually decreased.
    e. for a short period of time initially, then gradually increased.

14. When the time-out from positive reinforcement procedure is implemented, it is recommended that:
    a. negative reinforcement be initiated.
    b. response cost also be implemented.
    c. the individual be locked in a non-stimulating room, so that supervision is unnecessary.
    d. the alternate environment be as non-stimulating as possible.
    e. the alternate environment be equally reinforcing.

15. Time-out from positive reinforcement and extinction are similar in that both procedures:
    a. are best applied in isolation without the use of any other procedure.
    b. are preferred to response cost.
    c. can be applied to reduce inappropriate behavior.
    d. can be used to strengthen appropriate behavior.
    e. use negative reinforcement.

16. Time-out from positive reinforcement and extinction are different in that, after the exhibition of the target behavior, the:
    a. environment in the extinction procedure remains the same but in the time-out from positive reinforcement procedure the environment changes in some manner.
    b. environment in the time-out from positive reinforcement procedure remains the same but in the extinction procedure the environment changes in some manner.
    c. environments remain the same but the time-out from positive reinforcement procedure is then used in conjunction with response cost and the extinction procedure does not use response cost.
    d. extinction procedure is terminated but the time-out from positive reinforcement is continued.
    e. time-out from positive reinforcement procedure is terminated but the extinction procedure is continued.

17. Time-out from positive reinforcement and response cost are similar in that both procedures:
    a. are used to strengthen appropriate behaviors.
    b. involve the ignoring of inappropriate behaviors.
    c. involve the removal of a specific quantity of reinforcers.
    d. involve the removal of reinforcement, contingent upon the exhibition of a target behavior.
    e. involve the removal of reinforcement for a specified period of time.

18. Time-out from postive reinforcement and response cost are
different in that:
    a. the response cost procedure produces consistent results
       with all individuals but the time-out from positive
       reinforcement procedure does not.
    b. the response cost procedure strengthens an appropriate
       behavior and the time-out from positive reinforcement
       procedure reduces an inappropriate behavior.
    c. the time-out from positive reinforcement procedure
       involves the withdrawal of reinforcement for a specific
       amount of time and the response cost procedure involves
       the removal of a specific quantity of reinforcers.
    d. the time-out from positive reinforcement procedure
       produces consistent results with all individuals, but the
       response cost procedure does not.
    e. the time-out from positive reinforcement procedure
       strengthens an appropriate behavior and the response cost
       procedure reduces an inappropriate behavior.

When you have completed the evaluation, check your answers with
the ones listed in the back of the book. When you are satisfied with
your retention of the material related to response cost and time-out
from positive reinforcement, please turn the page to begin work on the
next chapter.

CHAPTER ELEVEN

TEACHING BEHAVIORS: SCHEDULES OF REINFORCEMENT

There are many different ways to determine when reinforcement will occur. The rules that determine when behavioral responses of a given kind are followed by reinforcement are called *schedules of reinforcement*. Each schedule is the basis for determining when responses are reinforced. The two major schedules of reinforcement are: (a) continuous and (b) intermittent.

When using *continuous reinforcement* each of the desired responses is followed by a reinforcer. If a recreation practitioner wanted to TEACH Lori the new skill of throwing a ball, the practitioner would reinforce Lori EVERY time she properly threw the ball. When a behavior is continuously reinforced (reinforced each time), the behavior tends to be learned more quickly. This characteristic emphasizes the importance of continuously reinforcing a behavior which is being learned for the first time.

A disadvantage to continuous reinforcement is that the behavior being maintained on such a schedule will extinguish rather quickly if reinforcement for that behavior is stopped for very long. The ideal time to use a continuous reinforcement schedule is when a new behavior is being taught. However, once a behavior has been learned the continuous reinforcement schedule is usually changed to maintain the behavior.

Characteristics of continuous reinforcement:

1. Reinforce EVERY correct response.
2. Used when TEACHING new behaviors.

Schedules which require reinforcement not to be delivered continuously are termed *intermittent* schedules. When intermittently reinforcing a behavior, reinforcement is provided OCCASIONALLY. This reinforcement occurs after some, but not all, responses. The intermittent schedule is more similar to the manner in which reinforcement is usually delivered in relatively unplanned daily activities.

117

Intermittent reinforcement leads to the behavior becoming highly resistant to extinction. Behaviors that have been intermittently reinforced will decrease much more slowly if reinforcement is stopped. This is an advantage when teaching a participant a behavior which will not be reinforced every time it occurs.

When using intermittent schedules of reinforcement, the reinforcer MAINTAINING the behavior will be more likely to remain effective all the time. This effect is due to the person not receiving a large amount of reinforcement in a short time. When a person receives a high frequency of a particular reinforcement during a short period of time, the item used as a reinforcer often loses its reinforcing properties and the behavior previously being reinforced will decrease. This occurrence, termed *satiation*, may more easily occur when continuously reinforcing a behavior. For example: Cathy may verbalize at a high enough rate to receive many marbles during a short time. Because of the high number of marbles Cathy receives, they may cease to be effective until Cathy has not received that reinforcer for an extended length of time.

Characteristics of intermittent reinforcement:

1. Reinforce OCCASIONALLY.
2. Used when MAINTAINING a behavior.

Following are ten examples of different schedules of reinforcement. Find the examples of continuous reinforcement and enter "CR" on the lines following those examples. Leave the lines following the other examples blank.

1. At the recreation center the after-school program for elementary school-age children includes group singing. Paula, a third grader, will sit with the group but often does not participate in the singing. Before the start of a group sing, the recreation leader decides to compliment Paula on an average of every two times she participates in a song. The leader decides to compliment Paula after the 1st, 3rd, 4th, 7th, 8th and 10th songs in which she joins in singing.

---

2. Richard, a new member of a park maintenance work crew, rarely reacts to efforts aimed at engaging him in conversation with anything more than one or two word responses. The crew

members would like Richard to converse for longer periods of time. The crew leader decides to encourage Richard with a pleasant smile when Richard has conversed for an average of ten seconds. The crew leader smiles at Richard after Richard has conversed for 8, 12, and 10 seconds.

3. A recreation therapist is attempting to teach James how to swim but James is a little hesitant about putting his face in the water. Each time James does put his face in the water, he is given several pats on the back and told he is making good progress.

4. Mary has signed up to learn archery during her stay at camp. On the archery range it is possible to accumulate wooden tokens for accuracy. When an individual has obtained ten tokens, they can be exchanged for a candy bar at the camp store. After every third bullseye, Mary is given a wooden token.

5. Storytelling is a popular feature of the summer playground program for young children. The stories are told in an open-sided shelter. Bradley, a kindergartner, is disruptive because he jumps up and runs about the shelter. In an attempt to help the storyteller, the playground leader decides to reward Bradley with verbal praise if he remains seated for a 45-second time period. Subsequently, Bradley will be praised for every 45 seconds he remains seated during a storytelling session.

6. A basketball coach is teaching his players to shoot left-handed lay-ups while jumping off their right foot. It is a difficult skill for beginners to learn. Whenever a player makes a left-handed lay-up off his right foot, the coach praises his efforts in front of the other players by saying "way to go" and then adding the player's first name or nickname.

7. Arthur is being encouraged to initiate conversation with other members of his leisure education class. After every second time Arthur begins a conversation with a classmate, he is given attention and verbal praise by the instructor of the class.

---

8. Wanda, who likes to chew gum, rarely completes projects in her crafts class because she spends so much time staring into space. The crafts instructor believes that Wanda can gain more benefits from the class if he can give her positive reinforcement for staying on task. Therefore, he decides to give Wanda a stick of gum if she spends three minutes on her project without staring into space. Wanda will receive an additional stick of gum for each three minutes she spends on her project without staring into space.

---

9. John, a resident in a home for the elderly, rarely participates in any recreation activities with the other residents unless he is coaxed into doing so by a staff member. In an attempt to get John to socialize without being coaxed, the recreation therapist decides to reward John with individual attention. The recreation therapist wants to reward John at differing times after he has played cards and plans to do so on an average of three games he plays.

---

10. The favorite toy of Betsy, a preschooler, is a huge, stuffed panda. Betsy is being taught to engage in cooperative play with other preschool children. The play leader plans to reward Betsy after she has engaged in cooperative play for an average of 90 seconds but predetermines that Betsy will be allowed to hug the panda after cooperative play periods of 75, 115, and 90 seconds.

Two major INTERMITTENT schedules of reinforcement are: (a) ratio and (b) interval. *Ratio* schedules are those schedules in which reinforcement is administered on the basis of a required NUMBER of responses that must occur before a reinforcer is delivered. A schedule in which every third response is reinforced would be a ratio schedule because there is a prescribed ratio of responses required for each reinforcement. An example would be the delivery of verbal praise after every third time Cindy catches a ball.

Ratio schedules of reinforcement are further divided into categories termed (a) fixed ratio and (b) variable ratio. When using a *fixed ratio* schedule, the NUMBER of responses required for reinforcement is SET at a designated number. This number does not change after each reinforcer is delivered. In the example of a fixed ratio schedule of three, three responses must occur prior to receiving reinforcement.

Characteristics of a fixed ratio schedule of reinforcement:

1. Based on the NUMBER of times a behavior occurs.
2. The schedule is SET at a designated number.

Return to the ten examples of different schedules of reinforcement. Find the examples of fixed ratio schedules of reinforcement and enter "FR" on the lines following those examples. Leave the lines following the remaining examples blank.

A *variable ratio* schedule of reinforcement also requires a NUMBER of responses per reinforcer. However, the number of responses varies after the delivery of reinforcement. For example: on a variable ratio schedule of reinforcement of 2 the participant may identify a leisure resource and be reinforced, make three identifications and be reinforced, then make two statements identifying leisure resources and be reinforced, etc. Notice that the number of responses required for each successive reinforcement changes but the "average" number of responses required is two. The number "2" designates how many responses, on the average, are required for reinforcement.

When using a variable ratio schedule of reinforcement, the therapeutic recreation specialist must plan in advance to insure that the NUMBER of responses required varies randomly each time, and the AVERAGE number of responses required is the same as the number specified initially, as opposed to developing the schedule "on the spot." This unplanned scheduling often results in a different average number of responses required.

Characteristics of a variable ratio schedule of reinforcement:

1. Based on the NUMBER of times a behavior occurs.
2. Reinforcement is delivered based on the AVERAGE number of responses.

121

Return to the ten examples of different schedules of reinforcement. Find the examples of variable ratio schedules of reinforcement and enter "VR" on the lines following those examples. Leave the lines following the remaining examples blank.

Interval schedules of reinforcement are schedules that involve the reinforcement of a response after the passage of some specified TIME. After each specified interval has passed, the next response is reinforced. For example: if 30 seconds is the specified interval, then the therapeutic recreation specialist would wait 30 seconds and then reinforce the first desired response occurring after the 30 seconds. The specialist would then wait another 30 seconds before reinforcing, and so on. Thus, on an interval schedule, the reinforcement is still response-contingent. *Response-contingent* refers to the fact that reinforcement only occurs when the appropriate response occurs. With this type of schedule there is a specified period of time which must transpire prior to the response being reinforced.

Two types of interval schedules are (a) fixed interval and (b) variable interval. *Fixed interval* schedules of reinforcement denote a consistent amount of TIME which must transpire between opportunities for reinforcement. The length of the interval DOES NOT CHANGE after successive reinforcers are delivered. For example: with a fixed interval of two minutes (the first presentation of the reinforcer would occur after two minutes), the recreation professional would use a watch or timer to determine when two minutes have elapsed. The professional would then reinforce the next desired response that occurs and then begin timing the next two-minute interval.

Characteristics of fixed interval schedule of reinforcement:

1. Based on a period of TIME.
2. The schedule is DOES NOT CHANGE.

Return to the ten examples of different schedules of reinforcement. Find the examples of fixed interval schedules of reinforcement and enter "FI" on the lines following those examples. Leave the lines following the remaining examples blank.

Variable interval schedules of reinforcement have a specified TIME which vary in length after the reinforcer is delivered. An AVERAGE interval is specified by the schedule and the length of any given interval varies according to this average interval.

Planning a variable interval schedule is similar to planning a variable ratio schedule, except the random numbers represent interval lengths rather than number of responses. The range of the interval

lengths is calculated the same as for a variable ratio schedule.
Characteristics of a variable interval schedule of reinforcement:

1. Based on a period of TIME.
2. Reinforcement is delivered based on the AVERAGE number of responses.

Return to the ten examples of different schedules of reinforcement. Find the examples of the variable interval schedules of reinforcement and enter "VI" on the lines following those examples.

Each of the ten examples should now be coded in some manner. If you coded examples 1 and 9 as VR, 2 and 10 as VI, 3 and 6 as CR, 4 and 7 as FR, and 5 and 8 as FI, you did the exercise correctly.

Any type of behavioral consequence may be delivered on any of the aforementioned schedules. When punishers are delivered on these schedules, the results are very different. A continuous schedule of punishment provides the most long lasting suppression of behavior. With continuous punishment there is also an increased chance that the person being punished will adapt to the punisher, resulting in the loss of its effectiveness. The suppression of behavior is less complete when using an intermittent schedule of punishment, and if punishment is stopped, the behavior will return at a rate similar to the initial rate sooner than it would with continuous punishment.

FIGURE 17

	Schedule is unchanging	Schedule changes
Based on number of responses	**FIXED RATIO**	**VARIABLE RATIO**
Based on amount of time	**FIXED INTERVAL**	**VARIABLE INTERVAL**

Please go to the next page to assess how well you retained the information presented on schedules of reinforcement.

TEST YOUR KNOWLEDGE OF *SCHEDULES OF REINFORCEMENT*

Directions: Read the following statements and identify the schedule of reinforcement that is being followed. Record the letter corresponding to the schedule of reinforcement that is described in the space provided after the example.

a. fixed interval
b. fixed ratio
c. variable interval
d. variable ratio

1. Lawrence is allowed to play cards for 15 minutes if participating in the exercise group for one hour. _____

2. Marian is given a pat on the back after every two correct verbal responses. _____

3. Carol is told she is painting very nicely once every two minutes. _____

4. The therapeutic recreation specialist smiles at Robert on the average of every three strikes he pitches in a baseball game. _____

5. Henry is given a toy on the average of every three times he follows the leader's directions. _____

6. James is given an apple after he attends the leisure resource session. _____

7. Sonya is given a check mark on the blackboard on an average of every three minutes she continues to work on her pottery. _____

8. Joseph is told he performs well after every ten lines he recites in a play. _____

9. The therapeutic recreation specialist has scheduled free play at 10:00 and at 2:00 for participants who acted appropriately during social games. _____

10. Approximately once every ten minutes one of the recreation staff tells William that he is effectively participating in the leisure resource group. _____

Directions: Please circle the letter that corresponds to the best answer.

11. Francis has enrolled in a swim class. He has never attempted to swim. You set up a program to teach him the new skill of putting his head under water. What schedule of reinforcement would be used?
    a. continuous
    b. fixed interval
    c. intermittent
    d. variable interval
    e. variable ratio

12. The therapeutic recreation specialist allows Sheila to ring a bell each time she correctly responds. This is an example of which of the following reinforcement schedules?
    a. duration
    b. fixed interval
    c. fixed ratio
    d. variable interval
    e. variable ratio

13. After extensive training, Theo has learned to participate in a group discussion session. To maintain this skill, what reinforcement schedule should be applied?
    a. continuous
    b. duration
    c. fixed interval
    d. fixed ratio
    e. variable interval

14. The following situation may more easily occur when continuously reinforcing a behavior.
    a. aggression
    b. deprivation
    c. generalization
    d. punishment
    e. satiation

125

15. The schedule of punishment that provides the most
    long-lasting suppression of behavior is:
    a. continuous.
    b. fixed interval.
    c. intermittent.
    d. variable interval.
    e. variable ratio.

Now that you have completed the evaluation, please turn to the back
of the book and check your answers with the ones listed. When you
have finished, please turn the page and begin work on the next chapter.

CHAPTER TWELVE

TEACHING BEHAVIORS: SHAPING

A common objective of many leisure programs is to encourage the development of new leisure behaviors in some of the participants by using reinforcement procedures. However, sometimes it is not possible to reinforce the desired new behavior because the program participants rarely demonstrate this behavior. The participants need assistance in learning the new behavior. A behavior modification technique that can be applied to help individuals develop new behaviors is termed SHAPING. *Shaping* is the development of a new behavior by reinforcing a series of behaviors that are progressively similar to the desired new behavior. With shaping, a new behavior can be initiated by first reinforcing a behavior that the person already exhibits that is similar to the desired new behavior. As time passes, the person is required to exhibit behaviors that are more and more similar to the desired new behavior in order to obtain reinforcement.

The shaping procedure involves a series of steps. With each successive step, the behavior required for reinforcement has to be more similar to the new behavior being taught than the behaviors that preceded it. Behaviors in the series of steps that were previously reinforced would then be subject to extinction. The final desired behavior is called the *terminal behavior*. The reinforced behaviors that are required to be more and more similar to the terminal behavior are called *successive approximations*.

There are five steps to follow in implementing a shaping procedure. Shaping requires that all persons applying the procedure have a clear understanding of what the terminal behavior is to be. Therefore, the first step in shaping is to describe, in overt terms, the specific TERMINAL BEHAVIOR. It is essential that the terminal behavior be described in observable and measurable terms to reduce the likelihood of possible confusion or misunderstanding concerning what the person is to do. If all people applying the procedure have the same understanding and expectations, then there should be consistency of reinforcement and progress should follow in an orderly manner. It is recommended that all of the characteristics (duration, frequency, intensity, etc.) of the terminal behavior be specified so that all successive approximations can be reinforced.

Shaping is a gradual process aimed at arriving at a new behavior. The essence of shaping is the reinforcement of successive approximations. The second step in shaping is to select, from all of the individual's behaviors, the behavior that will serve as the STARTING POINT on the road to achieving the terminal behavior. The individual must already engage in some form of behavior, no matter how rudimentary, that resembles the terminal behavior. That behavior can serve as the starting point. The starting behavior should be one that carries some assurance that it will occur with enough frequency during training sessions so that it can be reinforced and then serve as the basis for a succeeding closer approximation of the terminal behavior.

The third step in shaping is to determine the SUCCESSIVE APPROXIMATIONS that will be reinforced. Sometimes it is difficult to decide in advance exactly which behaviors to require as successive approximations. Because the participant's behavior may change slowly in very small amounts, or more quickly in large amounts, the person applying the shaping procedure often does not have the information necessary to predict exactly how much of a change to require. In such cases, it is appropriate to use professional judgment to arrive at an "on the spot" decision to determine which behaviors to accept as successive approximations and thus which behaviors to reinforce. However, tentative decisions concerning which small behavior changes to accept as successive approximations can be made prior to the implementation of the shaping procedure.

The fourth step in shaping is to proceed at the OPTIMUM PACE. This step requires accurate monitoring of the process and sound decisions based on the available data. The shaping procedure cannot be hurried, for there is a strong possibility that a successive approximation will not be fully established before moving on to the next one. If this occurs, the previous successive approximation may be lost through extinction before the new successive approximation is established through reinforcement. This is a serious obstacle in shaping.

Optimum pace also refers to the differences between successive approximations; that is, the amount or degree of change between the behaviors. Shaping should progress with behavior changes that proceed in a positive direction but are small enough to ensure their mastery by the participant. Otherwise, there is again the possibility that the previous successive approximation will be lost through extinction before the new successive approximation is established.

If the participant is unable to achieve a new successive approximation, it is probably due to being required to move too quickly through successive approximations or to make too large a jump between them. If this is the case, an earlier approximation that was firmly established should be re-established in the participant and the procedure then modified as it moves forward. On some occasions, when the participant does not engage in the required behavior, it is possible to give the participant a small amount of the reinforcer to see if this will bring about the required behavior, a process known as *reinforcer sampling*. Reinforcer sampling has been used with success in many cases. The potential danger in reinforcer sampling is that the participant may be reinforced for not engaging in the required behavior. However, this possibility can be controlled by providing only small amounts of the reinforcer. The remainder of the reinforcer can be provided after the required behavioral response.

The fifth step in the shaping procedure is one that is done simultaneously with the other steps. It is providing (to establish a new successive approximation) and withholding (to extinguish a previous approximation) REINFORCEMENT. Every time a successive approximation is exhibited it should be reinforced. Because it is a new behavior that is being taught to the participant, a continuous schedule of reinforcement should be applied.

For purposes of review, indicate the proper order of the steps of the shaping procedure.

1. _____

2. _____

3. _____

4. _____

5 _____

Your responses should be the same as the characteristics listed below.

Characteristics of the shaping procedure:

1. Specify a behaviorally defined TERMINAL BEHAVIOR.
2. Select the STARTING POINT.
3. Identify and accept SUCCESSIVE APPROXIMATIONS to the terminal behavior.
4. Proceed at the OPTIMUM PACE.
5. REINFORCE appropriately.

Now that you have completed the section related to shaping, please go to the next page and evaluate your retention of the material.

TEST YOUR KNOWLEDGE OF *SHAPING*

Directions: Please circle the letter that corresponds to the best answer.

1. What should the recreation leader reinforce when Thomas is being taught the new skill of rowing a boat?
   a. incompatible behaviors of the new skill
   b. previously learned tasks
   c. skills related to the new skill
   d. successive approximations of the new skill
   e. the total task

2. Once a substep has been learned and reinforced a specified number of times during a shaping program, what should the therapeutic recreation specialist do?
   a. generalize the learned step
   b. go back and reinforce that substep
   c. ignore the appropriate behavior
   d. incorporate the next step
   e. specify the target behavior

3. You have observed that Susan walks around the gymnasium rather than participating in the recreation program. What should be the first step in developing a shaping program for Susan?
   a. chain small steps together
   b. decide on a criterion for evaluation
   c. develop a sequenced plan
   d. reinforce successive approximations
   e. specify the target behavior

4. What is the term used to describe the reinforced behaviors that are required to be more and more similar to the target behavior while shaping a behavior?
   a. learned steps
   b. sequential plans
   c. successive approximations
   d. task analysis
   e. total tasks

5. Which of the following is an example of shaping a behavior if reinforcement is given to the participant after each of the following steps:
   a. enters activity room, writes name, is praised by the leader
   b. picks up pen, sets pen down, touches pen, makes marks on paper
   c. touches pen, lifts pen, rests pen point on paper, makes mark on paper
   d. writes name, is praised by leader, participant smiles
   e. writes with pen, writes with pencil, writes with crayons

6. What is the purpose of shaping?
   a. develop a new behavior.
   b. eliminate the need for extinction.
   c. gradually weaken an inappropriate behavior.
   d. improve a participant's physical condition.
   e. rapidly weaken an inappropriate behavior.

7. What is involved in the shaping procedure?
   a. a series of exercises aimed at improving physical fitness.
   b. a series of steps aimed at the gradual extinction of an inappropriate behavior.
   c. punishment of inappropriate behavior in conjunction with negative reinforcement of a desired behavior.
   d. punishment of inappropriate behavior in conjunction with positive reinforcement of a desired behavior.
   e. the reinforcement of a series of behavior that are progressively similar to the desired new behavior.

8. What is the final desired behavior called during the shaping process?
   a. positive behavior.
   b. shaping behavior.
   c. successive behavior.
   d. target behavior.
   e. terminal behavior.

9. What are successive approximations?
   a. behavior modification training sessions that take place on consecutive days.
   b. behaviors that bear no resemblance to the final desired behavior.
   c. reinforced behaviors that are required to be progressively similar to the final desired behavior.
   d. reinforcers that are applied in rapid succession.
   e. reinforcers that are somewhat similar to the positive reinforcer being applied.

10. What is the first step in implementing a shaping procedure?
   a. punish inappropriate behavior.
   b. put an end to successive approximations.
   c. use covert terms to describe the final desired behavior.
   d. use negative reinforcement to eliminate the inappropriate behavior.
   e. use overt terms to describe the final desired behavior.

11. When selecting a starting behavior in the shaping procedure the behavior should:
   a. be negatively reinforced so that it will weaken gradually.
   b. be rapidly weakened by punishment so that reinforcement of future behaviors that are similar to the final desired behavior can begin.
   c. bear no resemblance to the final desired behavior in order to avoid confusing the participant.
   d. not be reinforced so that substitute behaviors can be quickly learned by the participant.
   e. occur often enough so that it can be positively reinforced and serve as a foundation for future behaviors that are progressively similar to the final desired behavior.

12. In the shaping procedure, once a successive approximation is firmly established, what should the previous successive approximation be subjected to?
   a. alternate positive reinforcers.
   b. extinction.
   c. negative reinforcement.
   d. positive reinforcement.
   e. punishment.

13. In shaping, what should a new successive approximation always be?
    a. extinguished.
    b. ignored if it doesn't weaken of its own accord.
    c. negatively reinforced.
    d. positively reinforced.
    e. punished.

14. If the shaping procedure is hurried, what is there a strong likelihood of?
    a. a new successive approximation will not be firmly established before the previous successive approximation is lost through extinction.
    b. alternative positive reinforcers will have to be utilized.
    c. negative reinforcement will be applied to weaken the starting behavior.
    d. the original final desired behavior will have to be replaced with an alternate.
    e. the participant will have to be punished in order to prevent inappropriate behavior.

15. In shaping, what should be the degree of change between successive approximations?
    a. be ignored because it has no relevance to the participant.
    b. determined beforehand and no deviation should be permitted.
    c. be determined by random choice to avoid rigid behavior patterns.
    d. progress toward the desired final behavior but be small enough to be mastered by the participant.
    e. progress toward the desired final behavior in large increments in order to simplify the process.

16. What does the phrase "reinforcer sampling" mean?
    a. giving a participant a series of positive reinforcers.
    b. giving a participant a small amount of the reinforcer in order to encourage the desired behavior.
    c. mixing extinction and positive reinforcement.
    d. mixing positive and negative reinforcement.
    e. testing the various reinforcers available to determine which one should be applied.

Now that you have completed the evaluation, please check your answers with those listed in the back of the book. When you are satisfied with the degree to which you have retained the information, please turn the page to begin work on the next chapter.

CHAPTER THIRTEEN

TEACHING BEHAVIORS: CHAINING

Chaining is another behavior modification procedure that can be used to teach new behaviors to program participants. A *chain* is a sequence of steps that must be completed to correctly perform a terminal behavior. Each correctly completed step serves as a stimulus for the initiation of the next step in the sequence. When the final step of the series is completed, the program participant is positively reinforced. The sequence of steps related to the performance of a terminal behavior is sometimes referred to as a *behavioral chain*. The process of identifying a series of steps and guiding the program participant through these steps over a period of training sessions is know as *chaining*.

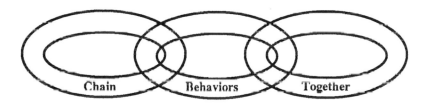

A procedure that facilitates the chaining process is called TASK ANALYSIS. *Task analysis* involves the precise delineation and sequencing of the components of an identified task or objective to facilitate individualized learning. By conducting a task analysis the therapeutic recreation specialist can systematically determine an instructional sequence of identified content that has been divided into manageable amounts of information. Task analysis allows the specialist to identify the content that can be taught through the chaining procedure. Through task analysis followed by the chaining procedure, the participant can learn an entire skill by initially learning segments of the skill, thus facilitating the acquisition of new material with a maximum amount of success.

Task analysis is conducted by examining the terminal behavior and considering the skills and abilities of the individual participant. Therefore, the therapeutic recreation specialist must continually examine the individual's progress when teaching the skill through chaining. If an individual is encountering difficulty progressing to the next task, it may be due to the fact that the task analysis was not COMPLETE. The current task analysis should be examined to determine if enough subtasks have been identified to completely cover the performance of the main task and identify any essential subtasks that have been omitted. Perhaps the individual has not been allowed to move at a fast enough rate through the teaching process and has begun to get bored with learning this task. The specialist may have delineated too many subtasks, included tasks that are not actually necessary to complete the terminal behavior, or repeated a subtask. Therefore, if this problem arises the specialist should examine the task analysis to determine if any of the subtasks are TRIVIAL, UNNECESSARY, or REDUNDANT.

The following is an example of a task analysis for playing electronic pinball.

1. Locates and stands in front of pinball machine.
2. Places dominant hand in pocket.
3. Grasps quarter using pincer grasp.
4. Pulls quarter out of pocket.
5. Extends hand toward front panel of machine.
6. Positions edge of coin directly in front of coin slot.
7. Pushes coin into slot by extending fingers.
8. Extends dominant hand toward small button on front panel.
9. Pushes button to activate machine.
10. Extends dominant arm toward ball release plunger.
11. Grasps knob using pincer grasp.
12. Pulls knob out by bending elbow.
13. Releases plunger by extending fingers.
14. Places one hand on flipper button on side of machine.
15. Places other hand on flipper button on opposite side of machine.
16. As ball approaches flipper, presses one or both.
17. Presses flipper to make contact with the ball.

Now that you have seen an example of a task analysis, try the following exercise.

You would like to teach a friend of yours how to bowl. To explain this task, you have decided to conduct a task analysis by segmenting into ten steps the skill of moving to the release line and throwing the ball. List the ten steps you have identified in the spaces provided.

1. _____

2. _____

3. _____

4. _____

5. _____

6. _____

7. _____

8. _____

9. _____

10. _____

If your steps resemble those presented below, it appears you are catching on.

1. Picks up bowling ball with both hands.
2. Puts fingers of dominant hand in holes.
3. Grips ball in dominant hand with the other hand under the ball.
4. Holds ball in front of body while standing three steps from the release line with feet together.
5. Points thumb of dominant hand towards pins, thumb up, wrist straight.
6. Holds ball forward with dominant hand and steps forward with dominant foot.
7. Lowers ball to side of leg and close to body and steps forward with other foot.
8. Draws ball back past body while bending knees and steps forward with dominant foot.

9. Brings ball forward while continuing to bend knees and steps forward with other foot just in front of the release line.
10. Releases ball in front of other foot six inches from the floor.

When chaining a terminal behavior, each step in the chain has a consequence that serves as a CONDITIONED REINFORCER for that particular step and also as an antecedent to the next step in the series. A *conditioned reinforcer* is any stimulus that was not previously a reinforcer but has acquired the properties of such by association with a stimulus that is a reinforcer. All steps in the sequence have this characteristic, except the final step. The final step in the chain is followed by the completion of the task. Task completion results in enhanced participation. Participation in many leisure pursuits is usually enjoyable and provides the necessary reinforcement for task completion.

For example, a therapeutic recreation specialist may decide to use chaining to teach a boy who has severe mental retardation to kick a ball to prepare the boy to play soccer. The initial phase of the chaining procedure is to identify the sequence of steps that must be correctly completed by the boy in order to perform the behavior of "kicking a ball." The action of kicking a ball can be separated into the following sequence of steps:

1. stand with weight evenly distributed on both feet
2. shift weight to right foot
3. step forward with left foot
4. shift weight to left foot
5. swing right leg forward
6. contact ball with toes of right foot

The opportunity to kick the soccer ball would serve as the stimulus for the boy to perform the first step in the sequence; that is, standing with his weight evenly distributed on both feet. Performance of this first step will serve as a stimulus for performing the second step. Completion of the second step in the sequence, shifting the weight to the right foot, reinforces the first step and acts as a stimulus for performing the third step. This phenomenon continues through all the steps in the chain until the final step is performed. Performance of the final step is reinforced when the boy has successfully kicked the soccer ball. The aforementioned example demonstrates the process of FORWARD CHAINING. *Forward chaining* involves teaching the sequence of steps in the order in which they will normally occur. The first step in the chain is taught first, followed by the second step and so on. Depending on the behavior to be learned and the participant who is to learn it, forward chaining can be an appropriate procedure to utilize.

A common way to teach a behavior that has been separated into a sequence of steps is called BACKWARD CHAINING. *Backward chaining* involves teaching the steps in the reverse order that they normally will occur in the chain. The last step in the chain will be taught first. When this step is performed at an appropriate level, the participant is then taught the next to last step in the chain. When the next to last step is performed correctly, the participant is presented with the opportunity to perform the last step (which has already been mastered). Completion of the last step of a recreation activity will typically result in an enjoyable experience and thus be considered to be a positive reinforcement.

In the example of the boy being taught to kick the soccer ball, backward chaining would be an appropriate procedure to employ. The final step in the sequence of steps was identified as "swinging the right leg forward, contacting the ball with the toes of the right foot." This is the step that would be taught first. It could be taught by the therapeutic recreation specialist placing the ball directly in front of the boy's right foot and prompting him to kick the ball. The correct performance of this final step would be followed by positive reinforcement. In this case, the positive reinforcement is the enjoyment experienced by the participant by being able to propel the ball. When the boy has demonstrated that he can consistently perform the final step, he would then be taught the next to last step.

The next to last step in this sequence was identified as "swinging the right leg backward." The therapeutic recreation specialist could teach this step by placing the soccer ball several inches away from the boy's right foot and again instructing him to kick the ball. The boy would then have to swing his right leg backward (the next to last step) in order to swing it forward and make contact with the ball (the final step). Performance of the final step would again provide the positive reinforcement. This procedure would be followed back through the steps of the chain. The final task for the boy to complete would be learning the first step in the sequence. When the boy has successfully mastered all of the steps in the chain, he will have developed the fundamental skill of kicking a soccer ball. He will have learned a terminal behavior and be ready to learn other new behaviors that will enable him to experience enjoyment from participating in a soccer game.

There are two major advantages associated with backward chaining that are not present with forward chaining. First, backward chaining guarantees that when teaching has begun for any step in the chain, the consequence of the step will ALWAYS BE REINFORCED. Second, backward chaining AVOIDS DISRUPTION of a previously established sequence of steps and consequences. Once a consequence has been arranged to follow a given step, it will always continue to follow the same step. This prevents the step from stopping due to extinction.

Advantages of backward chaining:

1. The consequence of the steps will ALWAYS BE REINFORCED.
2. AVOIDS DISRUPTION of previously established steps.

Although chaining and shaping are both procedures used to teach new behaviors, there are substantial differences between the two. In shaping, the successive approximations are discarded (through extinction) as progress is made toward the terminal behavior. When the terminal behavior is established, the successive approximations are no longer needed. In chaining, all of the steps are essential in order to perform the terminal behavior correctly and thus they are all retained. In shaping, the learning proceeds in a forward mode; the sequence of tasks is from first to last. In chaining, the process is most often reversed.

Shaping is the appropriate procedure to employ when the new behavior to be learned is a refinement of an approximation or a modification of a form of a behavior (length, intensity, vigor, etc.). Shaping can be done in a more loosely structured environment because approximations of the behavior are acceptable; correct performance of a step in a series of steps is not required in shaping as it is in chaining. Chaining can be employed when the behavior to be learned is capable of being separated in a series of discrete steps. Chaining requires a more structured environment because the steps must be performed correctly; approximations of the step generally are not adequate for mastery of the behavior.

Please go to the next page and evaluate how well you retained the information presented on chaining.

TEST YOUR KNOWLEDGE OF *CHAINING*

Directions: Please circle the letter that corresponds to the best answer.

1. Brenda performs the individual steps needed for her to go to a movie; however, she does not complete them in the correct sequence. After identifying six steps involved in going to a movie, you decide to teach her these skills. You may choose to teach Brenda by having her perform step 1 and then assist her with steps 2-6. Once she has learned this step you will require her to perform steps 1 and 2. You will then assist her with steps 3-6. What teaching procedure have you implemented if you continue in this manner?
   a. alternate shaping
   b. backward chaining
   c. forward chaining
   d. graduated guidance
   e. longitudinal cuing

2. Ben has learned to ride public transportation, read at the library, and check out a book. What will be your next step in teaching Ben to independently use the community library?
   a. accelerate the three skills
   b. chain the three skills
   c. fade the three skills
   d. reinforce the three skills
   e. shape the three skills

Directions: Based on the next paragraph, please answer the two associated questions.

Calvin was in a woodworking session. To complete his project he had to pick up a board, lay it in a jig, drill a hole in it, insert a dowel, then give it to the leader. A problem arose one day when the drill bit was dull and would not make the hole in the wood. Calvin picked up a board, laid it in the jig, attempted to drill a hole, then stopped. After stopping he simply sat at his work area and looked around the room.

3. What was the reinforcement that usually followed the entire behavioral chain?
   a. drilling the hole
   b. giving the project to the leader
   c. inserting the dowel
   d. laying the board in the jig
   e. picking up the board

4. What was the antecedent condition which did not occur in order for Calvin to complete the chain?
   a. drilling the hole
   b. giving the project to the leader
   c. inserting the dowel
   d. laying the board in the jig
   e. picking up the board

5. What is the purpose of chaining?
   a. allow program participants an opportunity to associate leisure with learning.
   b. develop a new behavior.
   c. extinguish inappropriate behavior.
   d. link conditioned reinforcement with inappropriate behaviors.
   e. link extinction with positive reinforcement.

6. A chain may be defined as a series of steps that must be accomplished to do what?
   a. connect extinction with positive reinforcement.
   b. insure that each behavior has an antecedent and a consequence.
   c. insure that leisure experiences are educational
   d. successfully perform a terminal behavior.
   e. weaken an inappropriate behavior.

7. What does the chaining procedure involve?
   a. associating leisure education with recreation activities.
   b. following a sequence of steps to weaken an inappropriate behavior.
   c. linking together several separate behavior modification procedures.
   d. the identification of a sequence of steps and guidance of a participant through those steps to mastery of a new behavior.
   e. the identification of a series of steps aimed at improving general fitness.

8. What is a series of steps that must be correctly performed to master a new behavior referred to as?
   a. a behavioral chain.
   b. a behavioral stimulus.
   c. a terminal behavior.
   d. conditioned reinforcers.
   e. conditioned stimuli.

9. What is a conditioned reinforcer?
   a. behavior that reinforces itself.
   b. physical exercise aimed at improving general fitness.
   c. reinforcer that can only be applied according to pre?-determined conditions.
   d. stimulus that has acquired reinforcing properties through association with a reinforcer.
   e. stimulus that intermittently has reinforcing properties.

10. What is backward chaining?
    a. a procedure that, because of its undesirable side-effects, should be used only if other methods have been tried and failed.
    b. a procedure that involves teaching the steps in a behavioral chain in reverse order to their normal occurrence.
    c. first applying positive reinforcement and then applying extinction.
    d. sequential steps taken to eliminate a previously learned behavior.
    e. the phase applied to the procedure when the participant is extremely slow in learning the required steps.

11. What is forward chaining?
    a. a procedure that first applies negative reinforcement and then applies extinction.
    b. a procedure that involves teaching a sequence of steps for a behavior in the order in which they would normally appear.
    c. a sequence of steps taken to punish an inappropriate behavior.
    d. stimulation of aggression and other undesirable traits in participants.
    e. the phrase used when the participant is exceptionally quick in mastering the steps required for a new behavior.

12. How are chaining and shaping similar? They both:
    a. are designed to teach new behaviors.
    b. improve a participant's general fitness level.
    c. rely on extinction of previously learned behaviors.
    d. rely on successive approximations of behavior.
    e. utilize extinction.

13. In the chaining procedure, the stimulus for the initiation of a step in the sequence is provided by:
    a. correct completion of the preceding step.
    b. extinction.
    c. negative reinforcement.
    d. punishment.
    e. shaping.

14. In the chaining procedure, positive reinforcement is provided to the individual:
    a. after the completion of the first step.
    b. at the discretion of the training staff.
    c. only if the individual is unable to complete the task.
    d. when the final step of the series is completed.
    e. whenever the individual requests it.

15. A major advantage associated with backward chaining is that:
    a. extinction can be substituted for positive reinforcement.
    b. punishment can be easily applied as a learning stimulus.
    c. the consequence of any step in the chain is always reinforced.
    d. the steps are taught in the sequence in which they naturally occur.
    e. the steps can be taught in any sequence.

Now that you have completed the evaluation, please check your answers with the ones listed in the back of the book. If needed, review the material and try the exercises again.

CHAPTER FOURTEEN

GENERALIZING BEHAVIORS

One of the major criticisms raised against behavior modification procedures is the inability of individuals whose behaviors have been changed by these procedures to exhibit their newly acquired behaviors in different environments and under different circumstances. Exhibiting newly acquired behaviors in different environments and circumstances is referred to as generalization. *Generalization* involves the exhibition of a target behavior (a) over time, (b) in a variety of situations or settings, (c) across different individuals, or (d) with similar materials. Generalization can also involve the exhibition of various related behaviors that are similar to the target behavior. Because generalization of skills does not often occur automatically, systematic procedures should be employed that encourage generalization. Therefore, a requirement of a training procedure should be the exhibition of target behaviors during conditions outside of the training situation.

One way to encourage generalization, that has previously been addressed in this text, is the idea of INTERMITTENT REINFORCEMENT. Remember that the systematic occasional delivery of reinforcers increases the likelihood that a behavior will be maintained. *Maintenance* of a behavior is the aspect of generalization that is concerned with the exhibition of a target behavior over time. Once a participant in a leisure program has learned a behavior, the practitioner should then gradually decrease the amount and rate that the reinforcer is being administered. As the practitioner decreases the reinforcer, the participant will be required to exhibit more of the desired behavior for a longer period of time to receive the same amount of reinforcement. For example, when teaching a girl to play basketball, the coach praises her each time she completes a pass to a teammate (a fixed ratio of 1:1). After she has successfully learned this skill, the coach decides to reinforce her on the average of every four times she completes a pass during practice (a variable ratio of 4:1). As her skills increase the coach then reinforces her on the average of every ten passes she completes (a variable ratio of 10:1).

In the above example the basketball coach systematically reduced the amount of reinforcement delivered, while increasing the frequency of the desired behavior. The systematic reduction or introduction of reinforcement or punishment is termed *fading*. FADING involves the gradual change of the antecedent or consequence of a behavior in order to encourage a behavior to occur in response to a partial or new antecedent or consequence.

The procedure of fading can be actively used to teach a variety of leisure skills. For instance, a recreation specialist is attempting to teach a man with motor coordination problems who does not currently paint, how to paint a picture. In preparation, the specialist traces a picture on easel paper. The specialist then places a paint brush in the participant's hand and physically guides his hand so that he paints the picture. After several teaching trials, the specialist begins to fade the pressure of her hand as the signal for painting. The specialist accomplishes this fading procedure by: (a) lightly holding the man's hand for several trials; then (b) touching her fingertips to the back of the man's hand for additional trials; then (c) pointing to the picture, and finally (d) simply giving the man the easel, paint, and paint brush. In addition, once the man is successfully painting the picture, the amount of the picture traced on the paper can also be systematically reduced (faded).

The fading examples above should sound somewhat familiar. The fading procedure is similar to that of shaping. However, there is a definite difference between the two strategies. Remember that *shaping* involves the reinforcement of successive approximations of a target behavior so that the demonstrated behavior gradually resembles the target behavior. When applying the shaping procedure, the behavior is changed. Fading involves the gradual changing of the antecedents or consequences while the behavior is maintained. Therefore, the application of the shaping procedure allows leisure service delivery professionals to initially teach a skill to their clientele, while fading facilitates generalization of these leisure skills.

The likelihood of generalization depends on various circumstances. The more SIMILAR two situations, people, or materials are, the more likely it is that the behavior will generalize. Therefore, one way to encourage generalization is to conduct training sessions in an environment that is as similar as possible to the environment where the behavior is ultimately to be performed. For instance, a therapeutic recreation specialist was going to encourage individuals to attend recreation activities in the community by teaching people to use the mass transit system. The likelihood of generalization of the skill to a variety of different buses would be increased if the training actually occurred on a bus, rather than in a large cardboard replica of a bus placed in a gymnasium.

Another factor that affects the ability of an individual to generalize the behavior involves the type of reinforcer used during the initial training of the participant. If the reinforcers used during the training of an individual are not available in other situations, the likelihood of generalization is then reduced. Therefore, whenever possible, reinforcers that are NATURALLY OCCURRING in the environment (typically secondary reinforcers such as social interaction and activity involvement) should be used when training leisure participants.

A problem arises when professionals are unable to identify any reinforcers other than primary items for some of their clientele. In such a situation, the professional may attempt to use the PAIRING procedure. *Pairing* involves the coupling together of two antecedents or consequences in an attempt to have one begin to assume the properties of the other. For example, a therapeutic recreation specialist who works on a pediatric wing of a community hospital is attempting to encourage a young girl to practice walking. He observed that the girl will only walk when she is given some candy. The specialist decides to use candy to reward the girl for walking. However, each time he gives the girl candy, he also administers social praise. He continues to pair the two consequences together in an attempt to have the social praise assume the reinforcing properties of the candy. Once the pairing has continued for a time the specialist gradually fades the candy while continuing his verbal praise. Finally, the girl is only receiving social praise for practicing her walking. The work of the specialist is not yet over. He now begins to fade his social praise until the child is independently practicing walking.

Complete the following exercise related to the application of generalization principles.

Directions: Answer the questions based on the following paragraph.

You have decided to improve the swimming skills of William so that he can independently use his community swimming pool. Currently, you are providing him with a hug each time he swims a complete width of the pool. To enable William to successfully reach the opposite side of the pool, you hold his stomach and provide him with physical prompts to move his arms, legs, and head correctly.

151

1. How might you FADE the assistance you are providing William?

_____

_____

_____

_____

2. What other reinforcer, that is more NATURAL, could you PAIR with hugging?

_____

3. How might you apply the idea of intermittent reinforcement in an attempt to have William maintain his swimming skills?

_____

_____

4. Where would be the ideal place to teach William to swim?

_____

If your answers resemble the following, you are gaining insight related to the concept of generalization.

1. How might you FADE the assistance you are presently providing William? *Gradually remove the physical prompts to move his arms, legs and head by replacing them with gestural cues and then allowing him to perform them independently. Subtly reduce the amount of pressure on his stomach with your hand. Now that you are no longer touching him, you could first simply stand beside him and then you could gradually move away until you are watching from the deck.*

2. What other reinforcer, that is more NATURAL, could you PAIR with hugging? *Verbal praise.*

3. How might you apply the idea of intermittent reinforcement in an attempt to have William maintain his swimming skills? *When he is able to successfully swim one width with regularity, begin reinforcing him after he completes an average of two widths (variable ratio). If he continues to show progress, move to a variable ratio of four laps per reinforcer. Continue this process by making him perform more while receiving less reinforcement.*

4. Where would be the ideal place to teach William to swim? *At the local community swimming pool.*

Remember the following guidelines for generalization:

1. Use INTERMITTENT REINFORCEMENT.
2. Gradually FADE reinforcers that are maintaining the target behavior.
3. Train in an environment SIMILAR to where the target behavior is to occur.
4. Whenever possible use NATURALLY OCCURRING reinforcers.
5. If unnatural reinforcers are used, PAIR them with natural reinforcers.

While keeping in mind the aforementioned strategies, go to the next page to test your knowledge of generalization.

TEST YOUR KNOWLEDGE OF *GENERALIZATION*

Directions: Please circle the letter which corresponds to the best answer.

1. Generalization refers to a behavior that:
   a. automatically occurs in a given situation.
   b. has been established in one situation and, as a result, occurs more readily in other situations.
   c. is an approximation of the target behavior.
   d. is generally appropriate for any situation.
   e. occurs more readily in one situation than in any other situation.

2. Maintenance of a behavior refers to a behavior that:
   a. cannot generalize from one situation to another.
   b. does not occur outside of a training session.
   c. does not require reinforcement.
   d. is exhibited over a span of time in a variety of settings.
   e. quickly extinguishes outside of a training session.

3. To facilitate maintenance of behavior, reinforcement should be delivered:
   a. consecutively.
   b. continuously.
   c. generally.
   d. intermittently.
   e. sequentially.

4. To facilitate generalization of a behavior, reinforcement should be delivered:
   a. consecutively.
   b. continuously.
   c. generally.
   d. intermittently.
   e. sequentially.

5. Fading is:
   a. a procedure used to eliminate an inappropriate behavior.
   b. the discouragement of intermittent reinforcement.
   c. the gradual diminishing of a target behavior.
   d. the planned introduction or lessening of reinforcement
      or punishment.
   e. the weakening of the intensity of a reinforcer.

6. Fading is a procedure that:
   a. can be used to influence either the antecedent or the
      consequence of a behavior.
   b. can only be used to influence the antecedent of a behavior.
   c. can only be used to influence the consequence of a behavior.
   d. has limited application; that is, it can only be used in
      a small number of situations.
   e. is more effective with a fixed ratio reinforcement schedule
      than a variable ratio schedule.

7. Shaping and fading are alike in that:
   a. a general resemblance of a behavior to the target
      behavior is all that is required for success with either
      procedure.
   b. both procedures involve gradual change.
   c. both procedures require fixed ratio schedules of
      reinforcement.
   d. both procedures require variable ratio schedules of
      reinforcement.
   e. both procedures use successive approximations of the
      target behavior.

8. Shaping and fading are different in that shaping involves:
   a. gradual changing of a behavior and fading involves gradual
      changing of the antecedent or consequence of a behavior.
   b. gradual changing of the antecedent of a behavior and
      fading involves gradual changing of the consequence of a
      behavior.
   c. gradual changing of the antecedents or consequences of a
      behavior and fading involves changing of the behavior.
   d. gradual changing of the consequence of a behavior and
      fading involves gradual changing of the antecedent of a
      behavior.
   e. punishment and fading involves reinforcement.

155

9. Generalization of a behavior is more likely to occur if the:
   a. natural environment provides continuous reinforcement.
   b. training environment and the natural environment are not alike.
   c. training environment and the natural environment are similar.
   d. training environment provides continuous reinforcement.
   e. training environment offers opportunities for fading and the natural environment offers opportunities for shaping.

10. Generalization of a behavior is more likely to occur if the reinforcers used in the training sessions are:
    a. also available in the natural environment.
    b. also used in the shaping procedure.
    c. continuous.
    d. only available during the training sessions.
    e. used in a variable ratio schedule of reinforcement.

11. Pairing involves the joining of:
    a. an antecedent with a consequence to promote generalization.
    b. continuous and intermittent reinforcement.
    c. fading and continuous reinforcement to promote generalization.
    d. the procedures of fading and shaping to promote generalization.
    e. two antecedents or consequences of a behavior so that one will take on the characteristics and effects of the other.

12. Pairing involves the joining of a:
    a. primary reinforcer with another primary reinforcer.
    b. primary reinforcer with an intermittent reinforcer.
    c. secondary reinforcer with a fixed ratio schedule of reinforcement.
    d. secondary reinforcer with a primary reinforcer.
    e. secondary reinforcer with a variable ratio schedule of reinforcement.

13. Which of the following is <u>not</u> considered to be a strategy to follow in an attempt to promote generalization?
    a. gradually fade reinforcers that are maintaining the target behavior.
    b. train in an environment similar to where the target behavior is to occur.
    c. use continuous reinforcement.
    d. when primary reinforcers are used, pair them with natural reinforcers.
    e. whenever possible, use naturally occurring reinforcers.

14. If a therapeutic recreation specialist implements a carefully planned process of reducing the amount of reinforcement used to sustain a behavior, the specialist is:
    a. following a variable schedule of reinforcement.
    b. generalizing.
    c. intermittently reinforcing.
    d. using a fading procedure.
    e. using an extinction procedure.

15. If a therapeutic recreation specialist uses food as a reinforcer of a behavior and links verbal praise with the food, the verbal praise becomes:
    a. a conditioned reinforcer.
    b. a generalized reinforcer.
    c. a token reinforcer.
    d. an intermittent reinforcer.
    e. an unnatural reinforcer.

Now that you have completed the evaluation, please check your answers with the ones listed in the back of the book. If needed, review the material and try the exercises again. If you are satisfied with your retention of the material, congratulations are definitely in order. You have successfully worked through the entire book. Congratulations!

CONCLUSION

Behavior modification is a learning process based on the belief that behaviors are developed and changed through the arrangement of environmental conditions that are the antecedents or consequences of behaviors. The fundamental notion that all people are able to learn and improve has provided the foundation on which the principles of behavior modification were developed.

Behaviors are continuously being modified through environmental manipulation. The intent of the text was to make professionals more aware of ways by which the environment may be manipulated to result in behavior change. With knowledge of these basic principles, professionals will be able to more systematically provide services that are intended to enhance the lives of people.

The manual was developed with the intent of educating professionals about the basic principles of behavior modification. The discussion was supplemented by examples, exercises and self-evaluations in an attempt to provide the reader with as many opportunities as possible to acquire information on procedures for changing behaviors. The situations described in the text were presented within a recreation and leisure context to provide professionals with examples that should facilitate direct application of knowledge and skills. The authors believe that a basic understanding of behavioral principles can allow practitioners to more positively interact with their clients. As the interaction process is enhanced, the ability to participate in recreation activities increases.

ANSWER KEY

INTRODUCTION TO BEHAVIOR MODIFICATION

1. b 2. a 3. a 4. c 5. d 6. e 7. b 8. d 9. a 10. a 11. b
12. e 13. b 14. a 15. a

DESCRIBING BEHAVIORS:

1. e 2. b 3. b 4. c 5. e 6. e 7. c 8. d 9. e 10. d 11. b
12. b 13. d 14. e 15. c

OBSERVING BEHAVIORS:

1. a 2. e 3. b 4. b 5. a 6. c 7. a 8. e 9. a 10. b 11. d
12. b 13. b 14. e 15. b

MEASURING BEHAVIORS:

1. d 2. b 3. e 4. a 5. a 6. e 7. b 8. b 9. c 10. a 11. e
12. d 13. c 14. d 15. c

UNDERSTANDING BEHAVIORS: SEQUENCE ANALYSIS

1. c 2. a 3. a 4. d 5. e 6. c 7. b 8. c 9. e 10. b 11. d
12. a 13. d 14. a 15. a

ACCELERATING BEHAVIORS: POSITIVE REINFORCEMENT

1. e 2. b 3. a 4. c 5. d 6. c 7. e 8. e 9. b 10. d 11. e
12. e 13. c 14. e 15. a

ACCELERATING BEHAVIORS: NEGATIVE REINFORCEMENT

1. ANTECEDENT: recreator tells Douglas to put materials away
   BEHAVIOR: Douglas puts the materials away
   CONSEQUENCE: Douglas escapes the recreator's nagging
2. ANTECEDENT: participants are disruptive
   BEHAVIOR: recreator turns the music off
   CONSEQUENCE: recreator escapes disruption

3. ANTECEDENT: Carol looks out window
   BEHAVIOR: Carol puts on her coat
   CONSEQUENCE: Carol avoids getting wet
4. ANTECEDENT: recreator coaxes Ralph
   BEHAVIOR: Ralph joins the activity
   CONSEQUENCE: Ralph escapes recreator's coaxing
5. ANTECEDENT: Gail cries
   BEHAVIOR: staff buys Gail a candy bar
   CONSEQUENCE: staff escapes Gail's crying

6. c 7. d 8. c 9. b 10. e 11. d 12. c 13. d 14. e 15. c

DECELERATING BEHAVIORS: EXTINCTION

1. a 2. b 3. e 4. c 5. e 6. d 7. c 8. b 9. a 10. b 11. a
12. a 13. c 14. d 15. b 16. d

DECELERATING BEHAVIORS: PUNISHMENT

1. a 2. d 3. a 4. d 5. e 6. d 7. b 8. b 9. e 10. d 11. a
12. d 13. c 14. e 15. c 16. e 17. e 18. d

DECELERATING BEHAVIORS: WITHDRAWAL OF REIN-
FORCEMENT

1. e 2. a 3. b 4. a 5. d 6. e 7. d 8. d 9. a 10. e 11. c
12. a 13. a 14. d 15. c 16. a 17. d 18. c

SCHEDULES OF REINFORCEMENT

1. a 2. b 3. a 4. d 5. d 6. b 7. c 8. b 9. a 10. c 11. a
12. c 13. e 14. e 15. a

TEACHING BEHAVIORS: SHAPING

1. d 2. d 3. e 4. c 5. c 6. a 7. e 8. e 9. c 10. e 11. e
12. b 13. d 14. a 15. d 16. b

TEACHING BEHAVIORS: CHAINING

1. c 2. b 3. b 4. a 5. b 6. d 7. d 8. a 9. d 10. b 11. b
12. a 13. a 14. d 15. c

GENERALIZING BEHAVIORS

1. b 2. d 3. d 4. d 5. d 6. a 7. b 8. a 9. c 10. a 11. e
12. d 13. c 14. d 15. a

GLOSSARY

Abscissa axis - the horizontal axis in a graph.

Acceleration - an interpretation of data on a graph that indicates a behavior is increasing.

Activity reinforcer - a secondary reinforcer, one which involves participation in some event.

Alternative positive reinforcers - reinforcers other than those that are being withheld.

Antecedent - an event occurring prior to a behavior which in some way influences that behavior.

Aversive event - an event present in the environment that is not desired by the individual whose behavior is to be reinforced.

Avoidance - performance of a behavior that defers or evades an aversive event.

Backward chaining - teaching the steps required to perform a specific behavior in the reverse order to which they normally occur.

Baseline period - a period of time during which a behavior is observed prior to the initiation of a behavior modification program.

Behavior - any observable or measurable act by an individual.

Behavior modification - systematic procedure that can be used to change an individual's behavior.

Behavioral chain - the sequence of steps necessary to correctly perform a specific behavior.

Behaviorally specific statement - a precise statement or description that depicts explicit behavior, including any condition or limitations that apply to that behavior.

Chaining - the process of identifying a series of steps needed to perform a specific behavior and guiding an individual through the steps.

Conditioned punisher - any stimulus that is allied with a punisher and becomes, through association, a punisher itself.

Conditioned reinforcer - any stimulus that was not previously a reinforcer, but has acquired the properties of such by association with a stimulus that is a reinforcer.

Consequence - an event that occurs after a behavior has been exhibited and in some ways is influenced by or related to the behavior.

Contingent consequence - a consequence that consistently follows the occurrence of a behavior and is not otherwise present.

Continuous reinforcement - application of reinforcement after each occurrence of a behavior.

Covert behavior - a private, internal event such as an emotion or thought that is not readily identifiable or measurable.

Deceleration - an interpretation of data on a graph that indicates a behavior is decreasing.

Deprivation - the withholding of a reinforcer for a period of time to make it more effective when it is applied.

Discrete behavior - a behavior that has definite and easily identified starting and ending points.

Duration recording - a system of observing behavior that involves recording the length of time the target behavior occurs during an observation period.

Escape - the performance of a behavior which results in the cessation of an aversive event.

Extinction - a procedure whereby a reinforcer that previously sustained a behavior is withheld for the purpose of eliminating that behavior.

Extinction burst - an increase in the strength, frequency, or duration of a behavior following the initiation of an extinction procedure.

Fading - the gradual introduction or withholding of a reinforcer or a punisher in order to influence a behavior.

Fixed interval schedule of reinforcement - a pre-determined arrangement for administering reinforcement of a behavior when it occurs for the first time after the elapse of a specific time period.

Fixed ratio schedule of reinforcement - a pre-determined arrangement for administering reinforcement of a behavior after it has occurred for a specified and unvarying number of times.

Forward Chaining - teaching the steps required to perform a specific behavior in the order which they normally occur.

Frequency recording - a system of observing behavior that involves recording the number of times the target behavior occurs during an observation period.

Generalization - refers to the likelihood that a behavior learned in response to specific stimuli in a specific environment will occur in response to different stimuli in different environments.

Intermittent reinforcement - a procedure whereby reinforcement is applied after some occurrences of a behavior rather than after each occurrence.

Interval recording - a system of observing behavior that involves recording the target behavior if it occurs during specified equal intervals or segments of an observation period.

Interval schedule of reinforcement - an arrangement that requires the elapse of a specified amount of time before reinforcement is delivered for a behavior.

Instantaneous time sampling - a system of observing behavior that involves recording the target behavior if it occurs at the end of a time interval during an observation period. The time intervals must be of equal length, but they may be distributed unequally throughout the observation period.

Negative reinforcement - a procedure that increases the strength of a behavior by removing or postponing an aversive antecedent, contingent on the occurrence of the behavior.

Ordinate axis - the vertical axis in a graph.

Overt behavior - observable and measurable acts or responses of individuals.

Pairing - the association of two antecedents or two consequences in an attempt to have one begin to assume the properties of the other.

Positive reinforcement - the presentation or delivery of a consequence that makes a behavior occur more often in the future.

Premack Principle - a principle that states that if two behaviors are linked together, the less frequent behavior will be reinforced by the more frequent behavior.

Primary reinforcer - an unconditioned reinforcer, one that does not have to be learned to be effective. Primary reinforcers include food, water, and other necessities required to sustain life.

Punishment - the presentation of an aversive event or consequence immediately following a behavior that leads to a decrease in the occurrence of that behavior.

Ratio schedule of reinforcement - an arrangement that requires a number of responses before reinforcement is delivered.

Reinforcement - the process of applying a technique that results in the strengthening of a behavior.

Reinforcer - any stimulus that strengthens a behavior.

Reinforcer sampling - presentation of a small amount of a reinforcer in an attempt to bring about a desired behavior.

Response contingent - delivery of a reinforcer only if the appropriate behavior occurs.

Response cost - the removal of a specific quantity of reinforcement from an individual.

Satiation - a condition in which a reinforcer has been provided for so long or so often that it has lost its effectiveness.

Schedule of reinforcement - rules that determine when or how often a behavior will be reinforced.

Secondary reinforcer - a conditioned reinforcer, one that is learned.

Self-reinforcing behavior - a behavior that is its own reward, it reinforces itself.

Sequence analysis - the process of precisely identifying a behavior and its antecedents and consequences.

Shaping - the development of a new behavior by reinforcing a series of behaviors that are progressively similar to the desired new behavior.

Social reinforcer - a secondary reinforcer that involves interaction between two or more persons.

Spontaneous recovery - the temporary recurrence of a non-reinforced behavior during an extinction program.

Successive approximations - in a shaping procedure, new behaviors that are progressively similar to the terminal behavior.

Target behavior - a behavior that is to be changed as the result of a behavior modification program.

Task analysis - the precise identification and sequencing of the components of a task, mastery of which is needed to learn a behavior.

Terminal behavior - the end behavior that is desired in a shaping procedure.

Time-out from positive reinforcement - removal of reinforcement from an individual for a fixed period of time.

Token reinforcer - an object that can be exchanged for a desirable item or activity that reinforces a behavior.

Variable interval schedule of reinforcement - a pre-determined arrangement for administering reinforcement of a behavior when it occurs after the elapse of specified and varying lengths of time.

Variable ratio schedule of reinforcement - a pre-determined arrangement for administering reinforcement of a behavior after it has occurred for a specified and varying number of times.

Additional Texts on Behavior Modification

Alberto, P. A., & Troutman, A. C. (1986). *Applied behavior analysis for teachers (2nd ed.)*. Columbus, OH: Charles E. Merrill.

Axelrod, S. (1977). *Behavior modification for the classroom teacher.* NY: McGraw-Hill.

Bootzin, R. R. (1975). *Behavior modification and therapy: An introduction.* Cambridge, MA: Winthrop.

Clark, F. W., Evans, D. R., & Haverlynck, L. A. (1972). *Implementing behavioral programs for schools and clinics.* Champaign, IL: Research Press.

Craighead, W. E., Kazdin, A. E., & Mahoney, M. J. (1981). *Behavior modification, principles, issues, and applications (2nd ed.).* Boston: Houghton Mifflin.

Ferster, C. B., Culbertson, S., & Perrott Boren, M. C. (1975). *Behavior principles (2nd ed.).* Englewood Cliffs, NJ: Prentice-Hall.

Gambrill, E. D. (1977). *Behavior modification: Handbook of assessment, intervention, and evaluation.* San Francisco: Josey-Bass.

Harris, M. B. (1972). *Classroom uses of behavior modification.* Columbus, OH: Charles E. Merrill.

Johnston, J. M., & Pennypacker, H. S. (1980). *Strategies and tactics of human behavioral research.* Hillsdale, NJ: Lawrence Erlbaum.

Kazdin, A. E. (1975). *Behavior modification in applied settings.* Homewood, IL: Dorsey Press.

Maher, C. A., & Forman, S. G. (1987). *A behavioral approach to education of children and youth.* Hillsdale, NJ: Erlbaum Associates.

Martin, G., & Pear, J. (1983). *Behavior modification: What it is and how to do it (2nd ed.).* Englewood Cliffs, NJ: Prentice-Hall.

171

Meister, D. (1985). *Behavior analysis and measurement methods.* NY: Wiley.

Peterson, S. K., & Tenenbaum, H. E. (1986). *Behavior management, strategies and techniques.* Lanham, MD: University Press of America.

Rusch, F.R., Rose, T. & Greenwood, C.R. (1988). *Introduction to behavior analysis in special education.* Englewood Cliffs, NJ: Prentice-Hall.

Skinner, B. F. (1953). *Science and human behavior.* NY: The Free Press.

Skinner, B. F. (1978). *Reflections on behaviorism and society.* Englewood Cliffs, NJ: Prentice-Hall.

Sulzer-Azaroff, B., & Mayer, G. R. (1986). *Achieving educational excellence, using behavioral strategies.* NY: Holt, Rinehart & Winston.

Sulzer-Azaroff, B., & Mayer, G. R. (1977). *Applying behavior analysis procedures with children and youth.* NY: Holt, Rinehart & Winston.

Sundel, M., & Sundel, S. S. (1982). *Behavior modification in the human services: A systematic introduction to concepts and applications (2nd ed.).* Englewood Cliffs, NJ: Prentice-Hall.

Tharp, R. G., & Wetzel, R. J. (1969). *Behavior modification in the natural environment.* NY: Academic Press.

Thompson, T., & Dockens, W. S. (Eds.) (1975). *Applications of behavior modification.* NY: Academic Press.

Vitiello, C. (1983). *Altering behavior.* Dubuque, IA: Kendall/Hunt.

Walker, J. E., & Shea, T. (1984). *Behavior management: A practical approach for educators (3rd ed.).* St. Louis: Times Mirror/Mosby College.

Wielkiewicz, R. M. (1986). *Behavior management in the schools, principles and procedures.* NY: Pergamon Press.

OTHER BOOKS FROM
VENTURE PUBLISHING, INC.

The Future of Leisure Services: Thriving on Change, by Geoffrey Godbey

Planning Parks for People, by John Hultsman, Richard L. Cottrell and Wendy Zales-Hultsman

Recreation Economic Decisions: Comparing Benefits and Costs, by Richard G. Walsh

Leadership Administration of Outdoor Pursuits, by Phyllis Ford and James Blanchard

Leisure in Your Life: An Exploration, Revised Edition, by Geoffrey Godbey

Acquiring Parks and Recreation Facilities through Mandatory Dedication: A Comprehensive Guide, by Ronald A. Kaiser and James D. Mertes

Recreation and Leisure: Issues in an Era of Change, Revised Edition, edited by Thomas L. Goodale and Peter A. Witt

Private and Commercial Recreation, edited by Arlin Epperson

Park Ranger Handbook, by J. W. Shiner

Playing, Living, Learning—A Worldwide Perspective on Children's Opportunities to Play, by Cor Westland and Jane Knight

Evaluation of Therapeutic Recreation through Quality Assurance, edited by Bob Riley

Recreation and Leisure: An Introductory Handbook, edited by Alan Graefe and Stan Parker

The Leisure Diagnostic Battery—Users Manual and Sample Forms, by Peter A. Witt and Gary D. Ellis

Doing More with Less in the Delivery of Recreation and Park Services : A Book of Case Studies, by John L. Crompton

Behavior Modification in Therapeutic Recreation: An Introductory Learning Manual, by John Dattilo and William D. Murphy

Outdoor Recreation Management: Theory and Application, Revised and Enlarged, by Alan Jubenville, Ben W. Twight and Robert H. Becker

International Directory of Academic Institutions in Leisure, Recreation and Related Fields (Distributed for WLRA)

Being at Leisure—Playing at Life: A Guide to Health and Joyful Living, by Bruno Hans Geba

Amenity Resource Valuation, edited by George L. Peterson, B.L. Driver and Robin Gregory

The Evolution of Leisure: Historical and Philosophical Perspectives, by Thomas L. Goodale and Geoffrey C. Godbey

Leisure Education: A Manual of Activities and Resources, by Norma J. Stumbo and Steven R. Thompson

Risk Management in Therapeutic Recreation: A Component of Quality Assurance, by Judith Voelkl

Beyond the Bake Sale: A Fund Raising Handbook for Public Agencies, (Distributed for City of Sacramento, Department of Recreation and Parks)

Gifts to Share: A Gifts Catalogue How-To Manual for Public Agencies, (Distributed for City of Sacramento, Department of Recreation and Parks)

Venture Publishing, Inc.
1640 Oxford Circle
State College, PA 1⁶⁸
(814) 234-4561